DEION SANDERS

★

BRETT FAVRE

D0067234

DEION SANDERS

★

BRETT FAVRE

RICHARD J. BRENNER

EAST END PUBLISHING, LTD.
SYOSSET, NY

Like all my other books, this one is dedicated with love to my two wonderful children, Jason and Halle; and to all the children in the world, may you always play in happiness and help to build a world that is free from fear, hate, and bigotry of any type.

I also dedicate this book to the spirits of Edouard Manet, Claude Monet, Paul Cézanne, Auguste Renoir, and Vincent Van Gogh: Thank you all for the colors, the hay stacks, the apples, and the starry nights. Thank you, too, for giving the world a new way to see and for making me look and laugh, too. Thanks, too, to Billie Holiday and her incomparable gift of song, and to Thelonius Monk, Dizzie Gillespie, and John Coltrane for their gift of amazing music.

Here's a long overdue thank you to Bob and Rob Tringali at SPORTSCHROME EAST/WEST. And once again, I thank all the wonderful people at Scholastic Book Fairs for their continued support, and Carie and Dave of Typewave—and Lisa James—for pulling the project through for me!

*DEION SANDERS*BRETT FAVRE*

First Printing July, 1996   ISBN: 0-943403-41-3

The cover photos were snapped by Rob Tringali, Jr. and supplied by SPORTSCHROME EAST/WEST

Cover layout by Jim Wasserman

Copyright 1996 by Richard J. Brenner —East End Publishing, Ltd.

Cataloging-in-Publication Data

920   Brenner, Richard J., 1941 Nov 14–
BRE   Deion Sanders * Brett Favre / by Richard J. Brenner. - Syosset,
        NY: East End Publishing, 1996

            96 pp: ill.,photos; 19 cm.
            Includes bibliography.

            Summary: Profiles two of professional football's superstar players, Deion Sanders, who also has a successful career in professional baseball, and Brett Favre, the National Football League's 1995 MVP.

            ISBN: 0-943403-41-1

            1. Sanders, Deion—Juvenile literature
            2. Favre, Brett—Juvenile literature
            3. Football players—United States—Biography—Juvenile literature
            4. Baseball players—United States—Biography—Juvenile literature
            I. Title
                                920; B; 796.332'092 ; 796.357'092 - dc20

Provided in cooperation with Unique Books, Inc.

Mr. Brenner is also available to speak to student groups. For details, contact East End Publishing, Ltd., 54 Alexander Drive, Syosset, NY 11791, (516) 364-6383.

This book is not authorized by either of the players.

Contents

Deion Sanders

1. Only One Like Him 8
2. Seminoles Star 15
3. Neon Deion 21
4. High Flying Falcon 25
5. Super Bowl X2 34

Brett Favre

1. Dreaming 52
2. Doesn't Anybody Want Me? 55
3. The Golden Eagle 58
4. A New Start 63
5. A Storybook Kind of Season 68
6. Great Expectations 74
7. Going for Perfect 80
Epilogue 87

Author's Letter 90
How to Write to the Author, Players, and Teams 91
Sources 92
Deion Sanders Stats 93
Brett Favre Stats 94
How to Order Books 95

DEION SANDERS

[Author's Note: For a number of years, many Native American groups have been appealing to sports teams to not use Indian names like "Braves" or "Redskins," or logos such as the racist caricature of the laughing Indian as depicted on the uniform of the Cleveland baseball team.

In support of Native Americans who feel that nicknames such as the ones cited above are demeaning, I have declined to use them in this book.

If you share my feelings that those nicknames are disrespectful, you should write to the teams and to the Commissioner of Football. Those addresses appear on page 91 of this book.]

1. Only One Like Him

Deion Luwynn Sanders, who was born on August 9, 1967 in Fort Myers, Florida, received his unusual name from suggestions supplied by some family members. But it was Deion's mom, Constance Knight, who added a little sparkle to the name by adding an "e" to his first name and a second "n" to his middle name. "Anything else just seemed too plain," said Deion's mom.

Fort Myers, which is situated toward the southern end of Florida's Gulf Coast, is an ideal vacation spot, especially for snow-weary northerners, and is a nice, comfortable place to live for some of its citizens.

Deion, though, didn't grow up in one of the better neighborhoods, but in a public housing project on Anderson Avenue, then and now a bleak pocket of poverty in a sun-drenched city which sits on the bright, blue waters of the Gulf of Mexico.

Drugs and unemployment remain the dual demons on the dangerous, mean streets where Deion grew up. The high rate of joblessness, the pervading sense of hopelessness, and the delusion that drugs can eradicate despair, loom like permanent dark clouds in the midst of the dazzling sunshine that beats down on Anderson Avenue.

The poverty-stricken neighborhoods that stretch across this nation, from Roxbury to Watts, fester like oozing sores in the midst of the richest country in the history of the world. It's tough growing up in those city centers, where crime is commonplace and drugs seem to offer both an escape from an ugly reality for users and an easy meal ticket for sellers.

The only way to avoid the allure that quickly leads to addiction and death, or a lifelong existence of despondency and dependency, is to have a dream, and the determination to turn that dream into a reality that allows you to escape the unforgiving steel trap that is always waiting to snap out another young life.

Deion was lucky that he developed a love of sports early in life and that he had the willpower to avoid the pressure of the pushers. "If it wasn't for sports, I probably would have been messed up with drugs," said Deion, who doesn't take drugs or drink alcohol. "I probably would never have used them, but I would have sold them. That was the neighborhood job.

"It would have been easy for me to sell drugs, but I always had to go to practice. My friends who didn't have practice went straight to the streets and never left them. Let me tell you something. The best athletes in the world end up at home on the corner. Oh you bet they do! I call them Idas, 'If I'd a done this, I'da been here today. If I'da done that, I'd be making three million dollars. If I'da practiced a little harder I'd be a superstar.'"

But they never do practice harder, they never do make the big money, they never go anywhere, and the only place they ever get to be a superstar is in the broken-down dreams in their own doped-up minds.

"They'll be standing on that corner until the day they die, telling you the things they would have done," adds Deion. "I see them all the time. Guys who were as fast as me when we were kids." And now their only move is to shuffle from foot to foot on the sad corner of missed opportunities.

Although there are dozens of routes out of Anderson Avenue—teacher, lawyer, or automobile mechanic, to name but a few—the path for Deion was sports, and his guide was his strong and loving mother. As one of Deion's boyhood coaches put it, "Either the streets will raise you, or your parents will raise you." And Connie Knight made certain that she would raise her son and not surrender him to the drug-infested streets of Anderson Avenue.

Deion's mom did lots of little things to teach him about staying clean and out of trouble. But one of the most effective lessons she ever taught him happened after she had gotten a call from the local police station telling her that Deion and some of his friends were sitting in a cell because they had been caught throwing bricks through the windows of an old shack. Instead of rushing down to pick up Deion up as quickly as she could, Deion's mom just let him sit. And sit. By the time Deion's mom went to take him home, all of his friends had already been picked up and he was sitting there crying and shaking. "I thought you forgot all about me," sputtered Deion, who had been taught a lifelong lesson.

Deion's mom did her job at home despite the disadvantages of being a single mother and having to work at two jobs for five years after Deion's father, Mims Sanders, became addicted to drugs and deserted his family when Deion was only two years old. The burden on Deion's mom didn't ease until she married Willie Knight five years later, but fortunately for her and her son, Mims's mother, Hattie Sanders, helped care for her grandson while her daughter-in-law was at work.

Deion started playing an organized sport after he joined a T-ball league when he was five years old. Coincidentally, the field was directly across the street from Lee Memorial Hospital, the place where Deion was born and where his mom was working at the time. Deion's mom took every spare moment that she had on game days to look out the window and watch her little boy play. "He always had a ball in his hand," recalled Deion's mother.

In 1977, when Deion was 10 years old, he joined the Pop Warner Football League. But he was so polite and shy that Dave Capel, the former coach of the team, didn't think that Deion was going to be much of a player. "Off the field he was so mild, you didn't know he could play football," recalled Capel. "But once he stepped on the field, he was different kid. He could do almost anything he wanted to."

Even back then, Deion was a double-duty threat, scoring touchdowns on offense, where the lefthander split his time between running back and quarterback, and on defense, where he blanketed the field from his free safety position. "He loved intercepting passes and he loved to tackle people," recalled Capel with a chuckle. "It was his way to pay back for all the times that he was tackled when he played on offense."

Capel estimates that Deion scored a total of 40 touchdowns in his three seasons on the team, including a trio of scores that rocketed the Rebels to a win in the 1979 Pop Warner League national championship game. "If we needed a touchdown to win a ball game, we'd give the ball to Deion and he'd run for a score," smiled Capel. "You coach your whole life and you only find one like him."

While Deion quickly became a neighborhood sports hero, the people that he looked up to when he was growing up started with his mother and then branched out to include "Dr. J" Julius Erving, the soft-spoken, acrobatic Hall of Fame basketball player, who currently provides insightful analysis of NBA games as an NBC television broadcaster; Hank Aaron, who hammered a major-league record 755 career home runs before becoming an executive with the Atlanta baseball team; and Muhammad Ali, the former heavyweight champion of the world, as well as one of the most delightfully outspoken personalities of his generation. Ali, who was for a time stripped of his title because of his principled refusal to fight in the Vietnam War, created a boastful but playful persona that allowed him to good-naturedly declare to the world, "I am the greatest and I'm also the prettiest." Ali also coined memorable phrases such as, "Float like a butterfly, sting like a bee," and devised poetic rhymes that attempted to predict the outcome of his bouts.

"When I was kid, I really admired Ali," smiled Deion. "I loved the whole idea of Ali."

Deion began attending North Fort Myers High School just prior to the start of his sophomore year. Somehow, his Pop Warner exploits had failed to catch the attention of football coach Wade Hummel, and at only 130 pounds Deion didn't look as though he would be a big factor on the football field.

"Deion was the skinniest, shrimpiest little kid you'd ever want to see," recalled Hummel. "He was a good athlete with a feisty attitude, but he was just too skinny. We thought he was too small to help us."

So for the first time in his athletic career, Deion spent a season sitting on the sidelines. But that situation didn't last very long, because Deion quickly made an impact, first on the Red Raiders basketball team and then on the baseball team. And before the start of his junior year, Deion hit a growth spurt, added on a little weight, and became an outstanding defensive back for the football team. "He was a great safety," recalled Hummel. "The other team didn't throw many passes into the middle of the field with Deion there, because most of the time he'd just pick them off."

What impressed Hummel, over and above Deion's natural abilities, was his willingness to outwork everybody else on the team. "Most high school athletes with talent don't work super hard in practice," contends Hummel. "Not Deion. He worked harder in a practice than anyone. He wasn't satisfied with just being good, he wanted to be the best." That attitude was the major factor in Deion's emergence as a three-sport high school superstar in his final year with the Red Raiders.

At the start of his senior football season, Deion was switched to quarterback to operate the newly installed wishbone offense, which is designed to create a series of offensive options and defensive confusion.

With his sprinter's speed and strong left arm, Deion was a decidedly unpleasant dilemma for opposing defenses, which would never know if he intended to hand the ball off to a fullback bucking up the middle, or fake the handoff and sprint towards a sideline where he still had the option of pitching the ball out to a trailing tailback, or faking that pitch and either cutting upfield himself or throwing on the run.

But Deion was more then a collection of bionic parts—he was a decisive decision maker while the play was unfolding and displayed such a smart sense of the game that he became the first signal caller that Hummel ever allowed to call his own plays. Deion delivered the goods for Hummel, passing for 839 yards while rushing for 499 yards. Deion, who doubled as safety, picked off four passes and earned all-state honors in a state that routinely develops some of this country's most outstanding football players.

Deion was such an outstanding college football prospect that he had scholarship offers from dozens of colleges and universities. Deion, bowing to his mom's wishes that he stay fairly close to home so that she could attend his games, finally selected Florida State University. And even though the Seminoles' Tallahassee campus is about 350 miles from Fort Myers, Mrs. Knight didn't miss a single home game during Deion's four years at FSU.

Deion was a standout backcourt performer on the basketball team, too, averaging 24 points per game as a senior, and earning his Prime Time nickname after his friend and teammate, Richard Fein, had watched Deion put on a dunkathon while soaring for 30 points in one particular game.

Deion also sparkled brilliantly on the baseball diamond, hitting over .400 and stealing 24 bases during his all-state senior season. "Deion is probably the most gifted athlete I've ever coached," recalled Deion's former baseball coach, Ted Ferreira, who also tutored Boston Red Sox outfielder Mike Greenwell. "He did things that can't be taught, like hit a little flair over first base, switch on the retrorockets, and run it into a two-base hit."

Deion had such outstanding baseball potential that the Kansas City Royals selected him in the sixth round of the 1985 amateur draft, despite knowing that Deion had already made a verbal commitment to attend FSU the following fall. The Royals tried to persuade Deion to forego going to college by offering him a $75,000 signing bonus. That would have been a tempting offer for most teenagers, especially one who had grown up without much money, and who, as a grade-school boy with his mitt on his hand, used to hang out at the Royals' spring training site and talk to the players every time he could. But, eventually, Deion decided to turn offer down. "I'm worth more than that," he told his mom—and entered FSU, where he was assured that he could try out for the baseball team after the football season was finished.

2. Seminoles Star

The Seminoles' coaching staff knew that they had recruited a gifted and versatile football player, so they asked Deion to decide if he would prefer playing cornerback or wide receiver, two positions where his exceptional speed would be a prime asset.

Deion, after spending the summer thinking about his decision, decided to concentrate on playing cornerback. Since he had spent the majority of his time in his final year of high school as a quarterback, Deion had a lot to learn about playing defense, especially if he wanted to make an impact at a football powerhouse like FSU.

Deion never did have a problem with working hard, but he did, at first, have trouble with being on time for meetings and practices. Mickey Andrews, who was the defensive secondary coach, quickly tried, unsuccessfully, to discipline Deion by having him run laps each time that he was late. Then Andrews, knowing that Deion wouldn't learn what he needed to know if he didn't take a disciplined approach, pushed a different button, and told Deion that if he was late again, he would be benched for a game. Bingo! "He wasn't late anymore," recalled Andrews. "Because he never wanted to miss a game."

Deion, who did double-duty work as a punt returner, wound up playing in every game except for the one that he missed with a broken wrist. And with three games to go he joined LeRoy Butler, who now plays for the Green Bay Packers, as a starting cornerback. Deion quickly showed that he belonged when he picked off a Tulsa pass at his own goal line and then used his speed to turn it into a 100-yard scoring dash, the longest TD run in school history. Deion then capped off the regular season by returning a punt for a 58-yard scoring jaunt against Florida University, one of FSU's archrivals. Deion closed out his freshman year in the Seminoles' Gator Bowl win over Oklahoma

State, a game in which Deion picked off a pass and also made a half a dozen tackles.

"He came a long way in a short time," said Mickey Andrews. "And he also did a lot of maturing. Sure, he had tremendous ability when he came here, but he kept improving because he was willing to work. Most great players are willing to commit themselves to improving. They take their talent and learn the fundamentals, master their techniques. What makes them great is their willingness to work to improve their abilities. Deion is probably the hardest-working player I've ever coached."

When the rest of the football team put on their cleats and reassembled for spring practice, Deion laced up his spikes and joined the baseball team as an outfielder. Although Deion's season was cut short by an ankle injury, he did start in the team's first 16 games, and he showed a certain ability by batting over .300 while knocking in 14 runs and swiping 11 bases.

It was obvious at that point in his life, though, that Deion was much better on the gridiron than he was on the diamond. And Deion, realizing that he might have a good shot at the National Football League in a few years, began working out with the football team as soon as his ankle healed.

That work paid big dividends for Deion, who began attracting attention as one of college football's top defensive backs during his sophomore season. Deion also showed that he could rise to the occasion in pressure-packed games when he made an extraordinary interception against the University of Miami, the top ranked team in college football and FSU's other archrival.

At the start of the play, the Hurricanes' All-American wide receiver, Michael Irvin—who is now Deion's teammate on the Dallas Cowboys—ran a stop-and-go pattern that put a lot of downfield daylight between Irvin, who kept going, and Deion, who came to a skidding stop. As soon as Irvin broke by Deion, the Miami quarterback, Vinny Testaverde, who had helped set

Deion up with a pump fake, threw what looked like a certain scoring pass to Irvin. But Deion, using his amazing speed and athleticism, raced down the field toward Irvin and at the last possible moment leaped up and snared the ball out of the air and away from Irvin's waiting fingertips. "He looked like Willie Mays making that over-the-shoulder catch in the 1954 World Series," said FSU head coach Bobby Bowden in comparing Deion's interception with the most famous and well-viewed fielding play in World Series history.

The season had ended and spring returned—but Deion's stroke didn't. Over the course of a full 60-game schedule he knocked in only 21 runs while his average fell to .267. Deion did, however, produced a truly amazing prime time performance one day when the Seminoles needed a doubleheader sweep to win the Metro Conference championship and the track team needed someone to run a leg of its 400-meter relay team. After the Seminoles had won the first game of the twin bill, Deion jogged over to the track meet and helped the relay team earn the second-place finish that gave the Seminoles squad enough points to take home the conference track title. "The entire team went over there to watch him run," recalled FSU baseball coach Dick Martin. Then Deion made Martin jump for joy when he laced a game-winning, two-run single in the nightcap that gave the 'Noles the conference championship and a ticket to Omaha, to compete in the College World Series.

Although Deion was disappointed with his own play in Omaha, as well as FSU's fifth-place finish, he quickly put his energy into getting ready for the upcoming football season. There was a lot of excitement the following fall after a number of football pundits picked the 'Noles as the top college team in the country, while *The Sporting News* designated Deion as the number-one college cornerback in the nation.

The 'Noles lived up to their billing through the fourth game of the season, a 31-3 mauling of Michigan State in which Deion put a muzzle on his future Falcons teammate, Andre Rison. Rison, the Spartans' All-American receiver, had thrown down the gauntlet when he said that Deion wasn't any more than an "average" defender. Deion rose to the challenge on the field, first, by holding Rison to a single short reception, and then by rubbing salt into the Spartans' wounds with a 53-yard punt return, which set up one Seminoles score, and then by picking off a pass that set up a second TD. After he had his day's play, Deion roasted Rison like a marshmallow. "He's just an *average* receiver," said Deion, as the sarcasm dripped from his lips. "I told him, 'I watched you on film, and I thought you were great. The film must have lied.'" Ouch!

It was the 'Noles turn to be burned the following week though, as they lost a one-point heartbreaker to Miami that knocked them out of the No. 1 spot in the national polls. Although FSU responded to the loss by stomping their way through the rest of the season–starting with a win against a Brett Favre-led University of Southern Mississippi team and ending with a win over Nebraska in the Fiesta Bowl—they never caught the 'Canes, who finished right in front of FSU for the top spot in the national polls.

As the spring approached, Deion decided that since his future seemed to lie in the NFL, he should drop baseball and run track, a sport which would keep his legs in better shape for his senior season with the Seminoles football team. The plan appeared to make a lot of sense, since Deion turned out to be such a strong college sprinter that he was named the Most Valuable Performer of the 1988 Metro Conference Championships after he won the 100- and 200-meter dashes and ran a leg on the winning 400-meter relay team. Deion even turned in a 100-meter timing that was good enough to qualify him for the Olympic Trials.

But then fate threw Deion a curveball in June, when the New York Yankees selected him in the thirteenth round of the

1988 amateur baseball draft.

Although he had decided to concentrate on football and hadn't played an organized game of baseball in more than a year, the temptations were far too great for Deion to dismiss. Secure in the knowledge that he could sign with the Yankees and still be eligible to play his senior year of football in the fall, Deion couldn't resist the chance to earn a relatively large sum of money for the first time in his life, or to entertain the possibility of one day wearing Yankee pinstripes and playing in the house that Ruth built. But there were two other factors that probably motivated Deion, even more than the money or the possible glory of playing for the best-known team in the history of baseball. One was the compelling challenge to see if he could reach the highest level in a sport that he had only really trifled with. The other was Deion's deep-seated need to explore every possible avenue and not let a stone of his life go unturned. Or, in simpler terms, Deion had been set to walk down a single road, but when the Yankees, in effect, presented him with a fork in the roadway, Deion opted to see if he could straddle both paths, rather than having to choose just one of them.

So Deion signed a two-year contract with the Yankees and spent his summer "vacation" on a whirlwind tour of their minor league system, from their Rookie League team in Sarasota, Florida, where Deion hit for a respectable .280 average in 11 games, all the way up to their Triple-A team in Columbus, Ohio, where Deion hit a wall. Deion's .150 average in five games against top minor league pitching was a clear indication that he had been promoted at a rate of speed far in excess of his limited experience or abilities. Although the reason for Deion's rapid rise up the Yankees' minor league ladder is not definitively known, it is reasonable to surmise that the overbearing hands of George Steinbrenner, the Yankees' principal owner, were pulling the strings.

Before Deion could get too embarrassed about his incredible shrinking batting average, he headed back to FSU for his final season of college football. Deion was a virtually unanimous preseason All-American selection, while the 'Noles were the early favorites to win the national title they had been flirting with for the prior three years.

But Deion's dreams of playing on the top college team in the country were swept away in the season opener by the Miami Hurricanes' resounding 31–0 victory. The 'Noles took out their frustrations on Southern Mississippi the following week, downing the Golden Eagles 49–13. Deion started the rout quickly, picking off Brett Favre's second pass of the game and then racing into the end zone on a 39-yard TD return.

Deion played so spectacularly throughout his senior season that he won the 1988 Jim Thorpe Award as the best defensive back in college football, while also leading the nation in punt returns with a 15.2 average. Then he closed out his college career in sensational style when, with 13 clicks left on the clock, he made a goal line interception that preserved FSU's 13–7 win over Auburn in the Sugar Bowl. "The bigger the game, the better he played," declared head coach Bobby Bowden. "But he played well all the time.

"The thing that made him different from most stars was that he loved practice. Even when he was playing baseball, if they didn't have practice that day and we did, he'd come over and get his pads on. Things like that won the admiration of his teammates. They never minded all the attention he received."

Deion also left a lasting impression on Mickey Andrews, the coach that he worked with the closest. "He may be as good a person as he is an athlete, and you can't say that about everybody. My wife still thinks of him like he's one of our own sons."

3. Neon Deion

In the spring of 1989, the Atlanta Falcons selected Deion in the first round of the NFL draft. The only players selected ahead of him were Troy Aikman, the No. 1 overall pick, who has gone on to lead the Dallas Cowboys to three Super Bowl titles; Tony Mandarich, who was grabbed by the Green Bay Packers, after a consensus of pro scouts had hailed him as the best offensive tackle to ever enter the draft; Barry Sanders, the 1988 Heisman Trophy winner, who was tapped by the Detroit Lions and who went on to be named the 1989 NFL Offensive Rookie of the Year; and Derrick Thomas, who was taken by the Kansas City Chiefs and went on to win the NFL Defensive Rookie of the Year Award.

Almost as soon as Deion was selected he was on a plane to Atlanta, to hold an airport news conference with a major contingent of the local and national media. Deion, who was arrayed in an amazing amount of jewelry, laid down a quick-witted, high-gloss rap that was just as glittering as the gold he was wearing as he designed to accomplish the twin ends of making headlines and dollars.

When he was asked about the size of the contract he was seeking, Deion's answer suggested a number that was so high it couldn't even be named. "There's going to be a lot of zeros in that contract," snapped Deion, sounding as though he had scripted the answer. "You're going to think it's alphabet soup or something with all of the zeros in there."

After taking a few more questions from the horde of competing broadcasters and reporters, Deion, deciding to bypass the questioners and speak directly to the people, borrowed a broadcaster's mike and announced with a smile, "Hello, Atlanta. This is Deion Sanders, Prime Time Live." Then he looked at his designer watch and gave his viewers a timecheck and a promise. "It's five minutes to eight, and the thrill is here."

Deion was continuing the process of creating a larger-than-life persona for himself, an enterprise that he had started when he had shown up for his final college home game in the back of a chauffeur-driven stretch limousine. It was an act reminiscent of Muhammad Ali. Like Ali, the real Deion is a thoughtful, caring, and generally soft-spoken person who prefers the privacy of his home and family—and the company of his wife, Carolyn, and their two young children, Deiondra Yronne and Deion Luwynn, Jr.—to the night life that is chased by so many other prominent people. But Deion, also like Ali, had decided that the way to the bank was to create an outsized Hollywood Hills Neon Deion. Although he has never liked that particular nickname, it was an almost unavoidably accurate image of the persona he was creating.

Deion was neither coy nor deceptive about his intention or motivation. "They don't pay me to be humble. Some people will come out to see me do well. Some people will come out to see me get run over. But love me or hate me, they're going to come out. I'm a businessman now, and the product is me. Prime Time. 'Prime Time' is the way I market the product, and I'll do what I need to do to promote that product.

"Do you think they pay Jim McMahon on all those commercials to be humble?" he asked, rhetorically, speaking about the signal caller who had led the Bears to a win in Super Bowl XX and gained national attention with his outspokenness. "Jim McMahon is not, by far, the best quarterback in the NFL. But, he is the only quarterback who ever made $10 million in one year off the field."

After the press conference, Deion boarded another plane and flew off to Albany, where the Yankees had a Class-AA team, to resume his minor league career. If he needed any confirming proof that his act was playing, he received it each time he came to bat in Albany and the scoreboard flashed,

"What time is it?" and was answered by its electronic self and a thousand screaming fans, "Prime Time."

The difference between Deion and the MTV-video version of himself that he was self-directing was clearly evidenced on his first full day in Yankee pinstripes. Deion had gotten the call up to the Big Show on May 31, as a temporary replacement for center fielder Roberto Kelly, who had incurred a minor injury. Sitting in the dugout prior to the game against the Seattle Mariners, Video Deion gazed at the enormous expanse of Yankee Stadium, baseball's greatest stage, and told reporters, "You sprinkle a crowd around me, and that's what I like. Then you'll see what I can do."

After the game—in which Deion actually did deliver a taste of what he could do on the diamond by throwing out a runner at third to choke off a Seattle rally before tying the game at 2–2 with a groundout RBI, and then sparking a seventh-inning five-run rally that carried the Yankees to a 7–5 victory—Deion revealed his true self. "I couldn't believe it. I'm thinking about Mickey Mantle, and about Babe Ruth and Lou Gehrig. I'm thinking, 'I'm 21 years old and I'm *really* here.'"

Deion wasn't there for long, though. Despite a few bright moments, including his first major league home run, Deion was sent down to the Yankees' Triple-A farm team in Columbus after barely hitting his weight in his initial 13 games in the big leagues. Although Deion was disappointed at being demoted, he accepted the decision like a mature professional. "I'm being paid to report there," said Deion, who had to know that he really did need some additional minor league seasoning. "I'll do what I have to do."

Deion did make steady progress at Columbus, hitting for a .278 average and knocking in 43 runs against top minor league pitching, while using his superior speed to swipe 34 bases in 117 games. So in September, when major league teams usually call up their most promising farm hands, Deion received word

23

to report to Seattle, where the Yankees were playing a series against the Mariners.

Deion joined the Yankees on Tuesday, September 6, and promptly threw his own homecoming party by drilling a pair of doubles and his second home run of the season. The following day, right in the middle of the game, Deion received the call from his agent, Steve Zucker, that he was waiting for ever since the NFL draft the previous April: the Falcons had agreed to a contract that would pay Deion $4.4 million over four years. So right in the middle of the game, Deion said some hurried goodbyes and took the first plane he could find that was pointed towards Atlanta.

4. High Flying Falcon

Deion arrived in Atlanta on Thursday, September 7, and announced that he was buying his mother a million-dollar home. "Whatever I needed as a child, she made sure I had," said Deion. "Now I want to make sure that she has whatever she needs."

On Sunday, September 10, Deion arrived in the NFL and announced that he was one in a million. *Explosively!*

Without any training camp and only two days of scant practice, Deion was sent into the game to field a punt by the LA Rams' Dale Hatcher. Just prior to the snapping of the ball, Deion, standing near his own 30-yard line, raised his hands to rouse the fans inside of Atlanta-Fulton County Stadium, then settled under the high, arching punt. He fielded the ball. He dropped the ball. He scooped it up and side-stepped the first two would-be tacklers as he quickly scanned the chaotic clashes going on in front of him while circling back and to his right. Looking side to side and back again, his darting eyes found a single narrow path of safety through the twisted tangle of bodies, and he followed his focus down the field, accelerated into an open space, and then high-stepped his way to a 68-yard touchdown.

That opening day return allowed Deion to become the only athlete to have scored an NFL touchdown and hit a major league home run during the same week. His singular two-sport spectacular also projected him onto the front page of *USA Today,* and the halftime show of the September 11 broadcast of Monday Night Football. P-R-I-M-E T-I-M-E!

Although Deion was on his way to becoming an NFL superstar himself, he was still starstruck when he met someone like Lynn Swann, the former Pittsburgh Steeler great who had done the Monday Night Football interview with him. "He was *here,*" said Deion. "Right in the same *room* with me."

"He's the real deal," declared Marion Campbell, who was

Atlanta's head coach. "I like this guy. He's a good person. He handles himself well in the locker room and he's a devoted work guy. How many people would have arrived on Thursday and got into it like he did? At first I told him I might let him run back a punt on two and he said, 'Coach, I want them all.' The bottom line is that he wants to win. He's got big-time speed and so much confidence. He'll be great."

By the sixth game of the season, Deion, who was running back kickoffs as well as punts, had gone from backup to starting right cornerback, and had begun his full-time disruption of NFL offenses. In only his second league game, Deion had continued his first-game heroics by picking off a Troy Aikman pass to preserve a 27–21 victory. And later in the season, he intercepted a pass from the hand of Joe Montana, who was the San Francisco All-Pro quarterback, while holding Jerry Rice, Montana's All-Pro wide receiver, to only 32 yards receiving.

Deion went onto earn All-Rookie honors from the Pro Football Writer's Association and *Football Digest,* and was also selected as the National Football League Players Association Kick Returner of the Year. And while Deion still had a lot of things to learn about pass coverage to be considered an elite NFL cornerback, he had already taken a giant step towards that goal.

●　●　●　●　●　●

After a short period of rest, Deion reported to spring training, hoping to build on the groundwork that he had laid the previous season, Instead, Deion kept bouncing back and forth between New York, where he started the season and compiled a .158 average over the course of three stops and 57 games, and Columbus, where he hit for a .321 average in 22 games. On September 24, the Yankees gave Deion his unconditional release, making him a baseball player without a team.

While Deion pondered the very real possibility of becoming

a one-sport athlete, he reported to the Falcons training camp, where he worked on sharpening his abilities and getting acquainted with a new head coach, Jerry Glanville, and the new defensive secondary coach, Jimmy Carr. Then Deion started his second NFL season with a roar by picking off a pass against the Houston Oilers and ripping off an 82-yard TD return, the longest scoring play in the league during the 1990 season. Later in the season, Deion dented the Cincinnati Bengals with a 79-yard punt return, and then he closed his sophomore season he way he had begun it, with a 61-yard interception return for a touchdown that helped Atlanta clinch a win over the Cowboys.

Although Deion had taken another large step towards becoming one of the NFL's top corners, his second season was more notable for its brilliant bursts then for its overall consistency. Deion, unsurprisingly, still had areas of his game that needed upgrading, principally stuffing the run and reading receivers' routes. Mostly what Deion needed, in attempting to learn what is, arguably, the most difficult of all defensive positions, was to keep on working and to acquire the experience that only time and playing could provide. "Every player with great athletic ability still has some work to do with techniques," explained Jimmy Carr. "But Deion is very intelligent and quick when it comes to learning. The thing he has going for him is that he wants to win and he knows how to go about it."

Unfortunately for Deion, neither of the big league clubs that he had played for seemed to have a clue about how to build a winning team. The two Yankee teams that he'd been a part of hadn't even been in wishing distance of a divisional title, and the Falcons hadn't played a postseason game in eight successive seasons. It didn't appear that Deion's luck was about to change anytime too soon after he signed a one-year, $650,000 part-time contract with Atlanta's major league baseball team, a team that had been the National League's Western division doormat for three successive seasons starting in 1989. (Atlanta switched to the NL's Eastern division prior to the start of the 1994 season.) The deal that Deion struck in January of 1991 allowed him to leave the team at midseason and report to the Falcons' summer training camp. But during spring training, Deion started to suggest that he was reassessing his professional priorities. "If it's August and we're in a pennant race and I'm here and playing well, I can't say that I'm going to walk away. I see myself, in the long run, as a baseball player. Football will last only a few years for me."

It remains unclear whether Deion—who had actually been assigned to play for Atlanta's Triple-A team in Richmond, Virginia—was actually speaking from his heart, or using the media to help him renegotiate his contract with the Falcons, while enhancing his long-term perceived value with the Atlanta's baseball team's general manager, John Schuerholz, and its field manager, Bobby Cox.

Whatever Deion's intentions may have been, the fact is that it was his splendid play in spring training that convinced Cox that he belonged in Atlanta's regular season opening-game lineup. And after the first few weeks of the season, Deion's performance drew raves from John Schuerholz. "He's been as good a player as we've put out there every night," said Schuerholz, the person who had drafted Deion in 1985 when Schuerholz had been the general manager of the Kansas City Royals. "He's played with fire, with aggressiveness, and he's been getting on base. He worked his tail off this spring to make our team, and we couldn't have asked any more of him."

Deion's hitting dropped off so drastically, though, that he was demoted to Richmond on May 23. After a month in the minors, where he hit only .262 while striking out 28 times in 29 games, Deion was recalled to Atlanta because right fielder David Justice was sidelined with an injury. But after spending another month being overmatched by major league pitching, Deion decided to report to the Falcons right before he hit his now-customary sayonara home run, a three-run shot that lifted Atlanta over the Pittsburgh Pirates, 8–6.

As soon as he reported to camp, Deion was delighted to discover that Jerry Glanville had decided to let him do double duty and spend some time as a wide receiver. Then Glanville put his plan into operation in an exhibition contest against the Tampa Bay Buccaneers, and Deion responded to the challenge by making a pair of catches, one of which was a gravity-defying leaping grab on a 52-yard pass play. "I want to get the ball in my hands," said Deion, who is always looking to exploit his talents and maximize his play. "I think everyone on the coaching staff knows that."

Three weeks into the 1991 season, Deion put on a Prime Time performance that helped propel the Falcons to their first win of the campaign. Deion turned the game around when he sacked L.A. Raiders quarterback Jeff Hostetler, forcing a fumble that was recovered for a touchdown, in addition to picking off a pass that thwarted a Raider drive.

Two days after the Raiders contest, Deion agreed to help the Atlanta baseball team, which was engaged in a down-to-the-wire divisional race against the Los Angeles Dodgers, as long as he didn't have to miss any Falcons games or practices. That began a frantic two-week period in which Deion commuted between games and practice sites by helicopter and plane, depending upon where he was coming from and going to. Although Deion wasn't actually called upon to do much more than pinch-run, he did enjoy the thrill of being part of a hard-charging Atlanta team that finally clinched the divisional title on the next-to-last day of the 1991 season. Deion was truly happy for his teammates, but he was disappointed that his contract with the Falcons wouldn't allow him to be included on Atlanta's postseason roster. Deion had to try to be content with being a baseball spectator as Atlanta beat the Pirates in the National League Championship Series before they lost a seven-game Fall Classic to the Minnesota Twins that ranks as one of the most exciting World Series ever played. "It killed me not to play because it was a big game. I haven't been in a big championship game since Pop Warner," complained Deion, who might have felt less bitter if the Falcons had been high flying instead of looking like they were about to limp their way through another losing season.

"The only way I have a chance to be successful in baseball is to give it a shot for a full season, and I have to do it soon," said Deion, who was likely feeling the weight of his .179 career average as well as his frustration at not being able to compete in postseason championship play. Then Deion turned his full focus on the 1991 football season and the continued upward arc of his gridiron career.

Included in his 1991 highlight reel was a 100-yard kickoff return for a TD against the 49ers and a midseason game versus Tampa Bay in which he was credited with five tackles plus a pair of intercepted passes on his way to earning his second NFC Defensive Player of the Week award. Three weeks after the Bucs game, Deion picked off another pair of passes, returning one of them for a 55-yard touchdown versus the Seattle Seahawks.

Deion's four-star performance helped the Falcons' stretch drive, which saw them win five of their last six games and gallop into the postseason for the first time in nine seasons. The Falcons were able to continue their run with a wild-card win over the Detroit Lions, before they wiped out against a Washington team that went on to capture Super Bowl XXVI.

Deion's regular season exploits—including six interceptions, which tied him for the NFC lead, 14 passes defensed, two forced fumbles, and almost blanket-like coverage—earned him a trip to Hawaii to play in his first Pro Bowl, the NFL's postseason all-star game which pits the American Football Conference against the NFC.

But neither his small taste of playoff action nor his Pro

Bowl selection could dampen Deion's desire to make his mark on the diamond. "I've had success in football, now it's time for me to accomplish a goal in baseball. I'm a good baseball player," said Deion. "But I can be a *great* baseball player."

In reality, Deion had had trouble lifting his baseball career off the launch pad, and it wasn't until the 1992 season—a season in which he used his startling speed to hit a major league-high 14 triples and swipe 26 bases in only 97 games while compiling a career-high .304 batting average—that he demonstrated the ability to suggest that he might actually develop into a decent baseball player. Despite his improved performance, Deion still hadn't proven that he would become anything beyond a fourth outfielder, before it was time to put baseball on pause and report to the Falcons.

Deion found a unique way to be spectacular in his fourth season with the Falcons by topping the Pro Bowl balloting as both a cornerback and as a kick-return specialist. Deion, who romped to a 99-yard return against Washington and a 73-yarder against the Buffalo Bills while leading the league in kickoff return average and total yards gained, posted a dozen plays that totaled 30 yards or more, including a 37-yard reception from quarterback Wade Wilson on which Deion recorded his first NFL score from scrimmage. "He's the greatest athlete I've ever seen" exclaimed Ken Herock, who was the Falcons' director of player personnel. "Deion can play wide receiver, he could play running back. He can do anything."

What made Deion's accomplishments even more singularly amazing was that in the midst of the season he commuted back and forth between the gridiron and the diamond for two weeks while trying to help Atlanta win the NLCS and 1992 World Series. And while Deion wasn't a factor in Atlanta's triumph over the Pirates in the LCS, he never shined brighter on the diamond than he did in the Series, as he led all hitters with a .533 batting average and drove in the winning run in one of the team's two wins against the Toronto Blue Jays. "He's a tremendous baseball player," said John Schuerholz. "You can see the excitement and energy level of the club rise when he plays."

Deion's improved performance during the '92 season, coupled with his torrid hitting in the four Series games in which he played, may have prompted him to make baseball a higher priority than football.

But the wide discrepancy between Deion's abilities on the baseball diamond as opposed to those on the gridiron were never more apparent than in 1993, a year in which he chose to play baseball on a full-time basis, up through and including Atlanta's surprising loss to the Philadelphia Phillies in the NLCS.

Despite his concentrated effort, Deion never gained a steady starting spot in the lineup, or posted numbers that suggested he would ever become anything more than a competent big league baseball player. But then he put on his shoulder pads and like Clark Kent metamorphosing into Superman, he stepped onto he field at the Georgia Dome to produce one of the most remarkable seasons ever recorded in the history of the NFL.

Prior to his arrival—which took place immediately after Atlanta had lost the LCS—the team was 0–5 and seemed to be simply hang-gliding through their schedule. But with Deion in the lineup the Falcons soared to six wins in their next eight games. Although Deion tried to downplay his role in the turnaround, his teammates and coaches weren't shy about revealing what Deion's arrival had meant for the team. "Things really came together for us when Deion got here," acknowledged linebacker Jessie Tuggle. "He sort of gave us the kick we needed." Head coach Jerry Glanville cut right to the chase when he commented, "He allows us to play the way we want to play. He gives us a chance to win. There is simply no way you can measure his value to this team. I just don't know anybody who has his kind of ability."

With Deion—who was named NFC Defensive Player of the

Month for November—at cornerback, the Falcons were able to neutralize some of the most talented players in the game and defeat the two best teams in the league, the Cowboys and the 49ers. In the Falcons' 27–14 upset of Dallas, Deion put All-Pro wideout Michael Irvin in his back pocket, holding the gifted receiver to a single, harmless five-yard catch. Deion also helped put the game on ice offensively, as he took a short pass from quarterback Bobby Herbert and turned it into a 70-yard TD reception. And when the Falcons nailed the Niners with a 27–24 come-from-behind win three weeks later, Deion went facemask-to-facemask with the incomparable Jerry Rice, and came away with a pair of picks off of Steve Young passes while keeping Rice safely out of the end zone. "We don't worry about the guy he's covering," said Glanville.

Deion was such an overpowering performer that he led the league with seven interceptions, despite missing the first five games of the season, and joined Rice as the only other player to gain unanimous selection to the Pro Bowl. "He's absolutely a great player," said secondary coach Jimmy Carr. "It's a fact. I played in this league for 10 years and I've been coaching since 1966. In all that time, he's the best I've ever seen."

Even with Deion in the lineup, the Falcons finished dismally, dropping their final three games and missing the playoffs for the fourth time in Deion's five seasons with the franchise. "I'm tired of would've and could've," said Deion, who was thoroughly disheartened at the inability of the Falcons to yield a competitive team. "I want everyone committed to winning and I don't think that we have that." Deion's impatience grew to exasperation after the Falcons weakened the outlook for the 1994 season by allowing some key players, including Deion, to become free agents. "I don't even know if I want to play football next year," said Deion, dejected by the Falcons' inertia and worn down by the constant grind of endless playing. "Maybe it's time to focus all my time on baseball."

5. Super Bowl X2

Deion had a super spring training in 1994, prompting Schuerholz to declare, "Yes, he's a great athlete, but it's his determination and competitive spirit that allows him to excel on the diamond and on the gridiron." But two months into the season, with Deion hitting .280 and leading the National League in stolen bases, Schuerholz traded him to the Cincinnati Reds for Roberto Kelly, the same player whom Deion had temporarily replaced in New York in 1989.

Two months after the trade, a contract dispute shut down baseball for the remainder of the 1994 season, setting Deion free to pursue his NFL opportunities. A number of teams, including the New Orleans Saints and the Miami Dolphins, offered him long-term, big-dollar contracts, but the 49ers won the Deion Derby with the shortest and lowest offer on the table—a one-year guarantee of just over $1.1 million. "I sat and weighed every possible offer and I'm a happy man," said a smiling Deion as he modeled his new red 49ers jersey. "I mean I'm thrilled to death because this is where I think I have the best chance to fulfill my dream of getting to play in a Super Bowl."

Almost before the ink on the contract was dry, some former Falcons teammates, including Jessie Tuggle and Andre Rison, depicted Deion as being singularly selfish. Although Deion felt betrayed by what he considered to be unwarranted criticism from people whom he considered friends, he shrugged off their stinging words. "The biggest key to failure is to worry about the unfair things that another man says about you," stated Deion before ending his comments with a poetic note. "I've got miles to go."

Deion, meanwhile, had absolutely no problems fitting in with his new teammates, despite the general perception that his sometimes flamboyant play would clash with the low-key, buttoned-down style of the 49ers, who believed in handing the ball to an official after a TD rather than spiking it into the turf. "He's a hard-working guy, and he comes to play hard," said Niners quarterback Steve Young. "I don't think we needed to make a lot of room for Deion, he just fit right in."

The 49er teammates quickly saw that Deion's high-stepping didn't stem from a need to glorify himself or demean his opponents, but was simply an expression of inner joy bubbling up and over, coupled with desire to pump up his teammates and entertain the fans. "I hate to see guys go out there and handle their business like it's only a job," said Deion, who started out on the right foot with his new team by earning NFL Defensive Player of the Week honors in his first start in a San Francisco uniform. "Sure, we work hard, but we are blessed, man, making a lot of money for something we're blessed to do. Have fun with it.

"I don't go and hold a ball right in someone's face, or spike the ball at someone's feet. I don't do anything to belittle another man, I do things to excite the fans, excite my teammates and try to take them to another level."

Which is exactly what Deion did while turning in such a stunning season that he was named the NFL Defensive Player of the Year. "Everyone wants to raise their level of play when there's a great player on the field," explained Niners free safety Merton Hanks, who had a field-level view of Deion's contribution, which included six interceptions, three of which were run back for scores of 73, 90, and 93 yards. "You want to show everybody that you can play just as well as he does. I think everybody's level of play went up."

Deion's play provided the defensive spark that helped lift the 49ers over Dallas, the team that had defeated them in the past two NFC championship games. And one game later, after the 49ers had drubbed the San Diego Chargers 49–26 in Super Bowl XXIX, Deion had his dream.

• • • • •

In certain ways, 1995 was a repeat of the previous season

for Deion, starting with the fact that he was traded again, this time from the Reds, for whom he hit only .240 in 33 games, to the San Francisco Giants as part of a multiplayer swap that the teams concluded on July 21. Although Deion got off to a slow start in the City by the Bay, he finished his season with a bang by hitting safely in 29 of his final 40 games with the Giants, to wind up with a .285 batting average for the season, despite being hobbled throughout the campaign by an ankle injury that he had suffered on May 31.

Deion missed six weeks of the season immediately after he initially suffered the injury, but then he refused to have corrective surgery performed until September 29, after the Giants had been officially eliminated from the possibility of postseason play. But nothing was wrong with Deion's left arm, which he used in September to sign a seven-year, $35 million deal with the Dallas Cowboys, one of the most lucrative player deals in the history of the NFL. When he had signed with the 49ers, Deion had put his competitive instincts first and money considerations on the back-burner. This time around, Deion had the best of all possible worlds.

The ankle surgery prevented Deion from making his Dallas debut until the middle of the regular season, and he never did seem to hit his stride. But in the postseason, Deion, like the stars over the Texas Panhandle, came out to shine. Deion began his Prime Time performance in a divisional playoff game against the Philadelphia Eagles by picking off a pass, catching a 13-yard reception, running back a pair of punts, and recording his first Cowboy touchdown on a 21-yard reverse play. Then, after the Cowboys gouged the Green Bay Packers in the NFC Championship game, Deion jump-started the Dallas offense in Super Bowl XXX by pulling in a 47-yard Troy Aikman pass that put up the first Dallas touchdown and sent them on their way to a win over the Pittsburgh Steelers.

But Deion does more on a football field than can ever be

measured by the numbers he generates. He is, without doubt, the most versatile and electrifying player of his time, capable of producing a touchdown in more ways than anyone who has ever played the game. "I think he definitely brings more than whatever the statistics show," confirms veteran coach Sam Wyche, "With him, there are intangibles that he brings to the table. There's always the constant threat of what he's capable of doing that you must account for. I couldn't respect the guy any more than I do. He's got everything."

Defensively, Deion dominates a game like no other player since Lawrence Taylor, the former New York Giant, who revolutionized the linebacking position while appearing in an NFL-record 10 straight Pro Bowls from 1981 to 1990. Deion's mere presence in the defensive secondary demands such respect that most teams will very rarely even throw to his side of the field. While traditionally, defenses are forced to react to what offenses initiate, when Deion is in the game, the offense has already conceded a certain portion of the field, reacting preventively to the damage that he is capable of inflicting. "I think he's the best cornerback in the league," said long-time NFL coach Joe Bugel. "I don't mean any disrespect to Eric Allen or Rod Woodson, but I think Deion is in a class by himself."

PHOTO SECTION

Deion with a Prime Time smile
courtesy of Dallas Cowboys.

Deion looks to drive the ball
E.W. SPORTSCHROME EAST/WEST.

Touchdown bound
courtesy of Atlanta Falcons.

Deion on defense in NFC championship game
Mike Powell, ALLSPORT USA.

Intense!
courtesy of Dallas Cowboys.

Brett smiles for the camera
courtesy of University of Southern Mississippi.

A Golden Eagle rolls out
courtesy of University of Southern Mississippi.

Brett scans the field as a Falcon
courtesy of Atlanta Falcons.

Brett scrambles out of trouble
courtesy of Green Bay Packers.

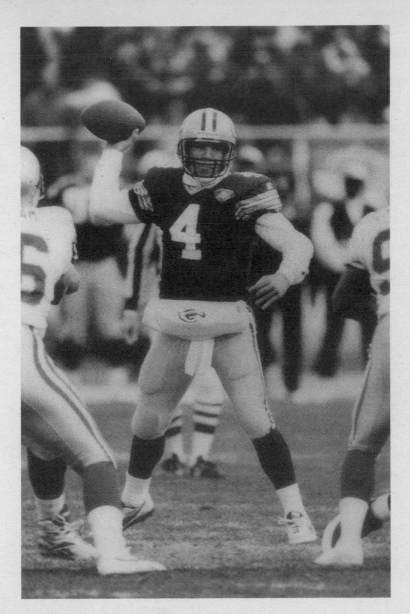

Set to win
Jonathan Daniel, ALLSPORT USA.

BRETT FAVRE

1 Dreaming

Brett Lorenzo Favre was born on October 10, 1969 in Gulfport, Mississippi, but was raised in a small town called Kiln, a hamlet of about 5,000 people that is only six miles from the blue waters of the Gulf of Mexico.

Brett, who is part Choctaw Indian on his father's side and was made an honorary member of the Mississippi Band of Choctaws, is part of a very close-knit family. He has such strong feelings for his family, and for the people and lifestyle in and around Kiln, that he still returns there each winter. "It's just everything you need," explained Brett. "It's not so much a town as it is a community, a neighborhood."

And the center of that community for Brett is the childhood home where he grew up with his parents, Irvin and Bonita; his older brother, Scott, who sells real estate; his younger brother, Jeff, who is a safety at Brett's alma mater, the University of Southern Mississippi; and Brett's younger sister, Brandi, who was the 1993 Miss Teen Mississippi. For Brett, the connection to his community remains intact as he returns to Kiln each winter. "People are surprised that I still live at home," said Brett, whose bedroom walls in his parent's home remain cluttered with the sports posters of his childhood years. "Well, I could be other places, but I can't think of a place I'd rather be. Where else could I have so much fun? And that's what this is all about—having fun." And when Brett recently decided to have a house built for himself, he had it built on his parents' land, just a short toss away from the family home.

When Brett wasn't playing, he was a conscientious student, who once had a ten-year stretch in school when he didn't miss a single day. Of course, playing hooky in the tight little community of Kiln was a near impossibility, especially given the fact that Brett's mom was a special education teacher while his dad was a teacher as well as the football coach at Hancock North Central High School. "Even if I was sick, I would just tough it out and go to school," grinned Brett, who even then was showing how determined he could be.

When it came to getting schooled in sports, Brett never had to leave the family backyard since his dad coached football and had been a college pitcher at the University of Southern Mississippi. Brett turned out to be a good enough baseball player to make the high school team when he was still in eighth grade. And Brett, who played third base, showed that he belonged on the varsity squad by pounding out a team-leading .325 batting average.

But Brett had always been more interested in playing football than he was in playing baseball. And he showed that he might have some special talent for the game as early as the fourth grade, when he won a Punt, Pass, and Kick competition in Biloxi, Mississippi.

Brett's fourth-grade teacher, Billy Ray Dedeaux, woke up at six o'clock on a Saturday morning to watch Brett compete. Sixteen years later, Brett nominated Dedeaux for the NFL's Teacher of the Month Award honors. "Brett chose me as his favorite teacher because he said I taught him values and hard work, and it paid off for him," said Dedeaux, who won the award in September 1994 and is still friends with Brett.

Brett began playing organized football as a receiver on his fifth-grade team. But on the first play of his very first game, Brett bobbled a pass and wound up falling on the ball, stomach first. The impact, which knocked the wind out of Brett and brought tears to his eyes, generated an immediate change of position.

"I told them I didn't want to be a receiver anymore," said Brett. "I was switched to quarterback, and it was like a jamboree. I had like three touchdown passes, and ran for maybe three more, and I said, 'This is for me.'"

From then on, Brett began dreaming of becoming an NFL

quarterback, like his boyhood heroes, Archie Manning, who was a Pro Bowl-caliber player for the New Orleans Saints, and Roger Staubach, the Hall of Famer who played for the Dallas Cowboys. Even in backyard games, as Brett called the signals he would pretend that he was Staubach, throwing a last-second, game-winning pass, or that he was Manning, eluding onrushing defenders and then racing into the end zone.

"I always looked up to those two guys and I said, 'That's what I'm going to do some day,'" said Brett, who as a sixth grader, wrote an essay on how he would like to grow up and become an NFL quarterback. Back then, of course, it seemed a very unlikely scenario that any player would graduate from a tiny town like Kiln to pro-football stardom.

"Even though I've finally made it, sometimes I still have to pinch myself when I think there's a little kid running around saying, 'I'm Brett Favre.'"

2. Doesn't Anybody Want Me?

Brett continued to reach for his improbable dream at Hancock North Central High School. Although it isn't always easy coaching a child or playing for a parent, Brett and his dad managed the situation without any problems.

"I wasn't overly talented," recalled Brett. "But my dad always pushed me to work hard and develop my abilities. Even now, he'll call me up after a game and tell me I could have run a play better than I did.

"He really kept me focused. The other guys on the team went home from school and forgot about football until the next day. But I had football at supper and football at breakfast, and that was fun for me."

Although Brett earned four letters at HNC playing quarterback and strong safety while also handling the Hawks' punting and kicking chores, his all-district performance didn't raise a blip on the radar screen of a single college coach. Part of the reason of why it was easy to overlook Brett was that he played for a minuscule school that fielded a mediocre squad. The other reason that Brett's play didn't attract the attention of college scouts was that his biggest asset, his right arm, was kept under wraps in the option offense that his dad favored. Irvin Favre placed such a heavy emphasis on the run that Brett threw only 55 passes during his four-year stint at Hancock North Central.

Fortunately, some neighboring high school coaches thought enough about Brett's ability to pass his name along to Mark McHale, who was an assistant coach and recruiter at the University of Southern Mississippi, the same college that Irvin Favre had attended.

"It was just a little luck and something that I liked about him," recalled McHale, who had a list of players to scout that didn't include Brett. "So I went to the schools who had players on my list, and I started to hear that Hancock North Central had a pretty fair country quarterback."

After hearing the story a few times, McHale decided to take a detour to Kiln and watch some tape of Brett. "So I sit down with Irvin, but all I'm seeing is tape of Brett handing off the ball. He only throws like three passes and nothing more exciting than a dump to the tight end and 10 yards to a running back." So McHale was all set to leave Kiln and get back to his list when he reluctantly agreed to stay and watch Brett play a live game.

Finally, while watching the pregame warm-ups, McHale got a hint at Brett's arm strength. "The kid can wing it," McHale remembered thinking. But during the game, even with McHale sitting in the stands and a college scholarship for his son probably hanging in the balance, Irvin Favre stuck to his long-time game plan and kept on calling running plays.

After the game McHale broke the news that he couldn't evaluate a quarterback after seeing him do so little, and he couldn't help but ask Irvin why he hadn't allowed Brett to pass more, seeing as the only college scout that was even likely to watch his son play was at the game. Irvin just looked straight at McHale and told him, "Because we have a kid who is a 1,000-yard rusher, and we keep winning with what we're doing." But before McHale could get out of town, Irvin convinced him to watch one last tape, which showed Brett throwing all of five passes. The first four were of the ho-hum variety, but the fifth one got McHale's football juices flowing.

"First he play-faked and rolled out to the right hash mark, right around midfield," recalled McHale, as though he was watching the play on a private rerun machine. "Then he stopped, planted his feet, and threw the ball into the end zone with smoke coming off it. I mean flames are shooting out, and it drills this little receiver for a touchdown — dang near kills the kid."

While that one exquisite pass convinced McHale that Brett

56

was the real deal, he still had to convince the decision makers on the USM staff that they should spend a football scholarship on an unknown quarterback. McHale's initial recommendation was, in fact, rejected, but he persisted and finally talked the quarterback coach, Jack White, into looking at the tape that he had brought back to the campus with him.

White was impressed enough to put Brett's name on the list of possible USM recruits, but it was the bottom name on a list that had 15 other high school quarterbacks above it.

One by one, though, the other signal callers either accepted a scholarship to a different school, or were whittled off the list for one reason or another, allowing Brett to receive the last football scholarship that USM had to give in 1982.

3. The Golden Eagle

Although Brett was off to USM's Hattiesburg campus, he wasn't going there as a blue-chip quarterback prospect. He had, in fact, arrived at summer training camp right after the 38th Mississippi All-Star Football Game, in which he had played as a defensive back while other, more highly rated quarterbacks ran the offense.

At the beginning of training camp, it looked as though Brett was also destined to play defense for the Golden Eagles, since he ranked seventh and dead last on the quarterback depth chart. Being the seventh quarterback on a team normally means that the player has about as much chance of getting out on the field in a game as the person who is in the stands selling popcorn. Even Brett wondered if he had the right stuff to make it at USM. "I know that I had only received the scholarship because the ball took a lot of funny bounces. And I really didn't think I was a good enough passer when I went up there."

But by the end of camp, after having had the chance to air out his arm and practice with the team, Brett had leap-frogged all the way up to number three on the depth chart. In addition to unveiling the fact that he had a powerful passing arm, it also became obvious that Brett had character as well as a fine mental grasp of the sport, which could clearly be traced back to his dad's tutoring. "He has tremendous poise, a good knowledge of the game, and a fine feel for running the football team," declared Jack White. "He also has a live arm and speed on the ball when he throws it."

Despite his climb up the chart and White's glowing praise, Brett didn't figure to play much, if at all, during his freshman year. He was thrilled just to have made the travel squad for USM's opening game at the University of Alabama. "It was exciting just to be on the sidelines," said Brett, who was awed by the sights and sounds of more than 75,000 mostly red-and-white garbed Crimson Tide fans rocking and roaring while their team squashed USM 38–6.

The following week, the Golden Eagles were again getting their wings clipped, this time by Tulane. So, in the second half, the coaching staff decided to see what Brett could do, and he responded to the challenging opportunity by throwing a pair of touchdown passes that propelled USM to a 31–24 come-from-behind win over the Green Wave.

Brett's performance earned him the starting role against Texas A&M, USM's next opponent. And while Brett was able to connect on another pair of scoring passes against the Aggies, this time it was in a losing cause. Brett and his teammates experienced some other tough times, too, including a 61–10 stomping by Deion Sanders and his playmates on the nationally ranked Florida State University team. But there were also lots of highlights, including a 65–6 rout of Louisville in which Brett threw a trio of TD tosses, and the season finale against Southwestern Louisiana in which Brett threw for a then-school record 295 yards.

But neither the wins and losses nor Brett's quarterback stats provided a true measure of just how far he had traveled since his senior season at Hancock North Central. In the space of a single year, Brett had transformed himself from a 17-year-old boy who was unwanted and unsure of his own ability, to a young man who was on the road to stardom.

Meanwhile, the USM coaching staff was realizing that it had stumbled onto a prize catch. "We got lucky," admitted former head coach Curly Hallman. "Let's face it, we ended up finding a four-year starter from a place that's kind of like the 'Dukes of Hazard,' minus the demolition derby."

Brett was dented, early in his sophomore season, though, when highly ranked FSU smashed USM 49–10. Deion Sanders sparked the Seminoles wrecking crew by picking off Brett's first pass of the day and turning it into a 39-yard return. "I rolled left and tried to hit my receiver on a hook pattern," recalled Brett. "But Deion stepped in front of the pass, and then he was just like *gone*."

Brett recovered from that drubbing, however, and led the Golden Eagles to a 10–2 finish as well as a win over UTEP in the Independence Bowl. As a passer, Brett had already started to rewrite the USM record book in only his second season, establishing new single-season standards for passing yardage and touchdown passes, while setting single-game marks for passing yards and completions as well as throwing a TD pass in nine consecutive games, yet another USM record.

Brett's accomplishments in his first two years at USM created a buzz about just how high the Golden Eagles quarterback would soar in his final two seasons. The expectations were so high that many preseason magazines predicted that Brett would be one of the top college quarterbacks in the country during his junior year. *Sports Illustrated* even sent a writer to USM's summer training camp to do research for a possible story. The assumption that Brett received was that if USM knocked off highly ranked Florida State in the season-opening game, the story would run. Brett did his part by throwing for a pair of TD passes and leading the Golden Eagles to a thrilling 30–26 upset over the Seminoles. As Brett walked off the field he was happily thinking, "I'm going to be in *Sports Illustrated*." But an SI editor, either by luck or inspired insight, withheld the story and then watched as USM followed their big win with four straight losses.

Brett, though, went on to post another superlative season, one which included 300-yard passing games against big-time college football powers Alabama and Texas A&M, as well as a 79-yard TD pass on the final play of the Louisville game that allowed USM to pull out a 16–10 win over the Cardinals.

"Amazing, just amazing," said Louisville's quarterback, Browning Nagels, of the play on which Brett first had to elude

Louisville's defensive tackle, Ted Washington. "I got a hand on him, but he slipped away," said Washington. "I got to him again, but he still managed to get the pass away. I couldn't even look. I just closed my eyes."

As the ball was coming down at the Louisville 30-yard line, a half dozen players jumped to meet it. One of them tipped the ball into the air, and USM's Darryl Tillman caught it on the dead run at the 25-yard line and raced into the end zone. "It was an absolute fluke," declared Louisville cornerback John Gainey. "Things like that aren't supposed to happen."

Spectacular plays, such as the one against Louisville, served as the inspiration for some legendary if not completely accurate stories about Brett. One of the tall tales started growing after Brett had drilled a game-winning 42-yard pass to wide receiver Alfred Williams, who turned around just in time to grab the ball. When he was asked how he knew when to turn around, Williams answered with a straight face, "Easy, I heard the ball coming."

Brett was looking forward to a strong senior season, which would also serve as a springboard to his aspiration of playing in the NFL. But Brett's dreams where almost derailed when, on July 14, 1990, he accidentally ran his dad's Nissan Maxima off the road. "I wrecked less than a mile from my house, coming around a curve I take all the time. My front wheel got caught in the gravel and slung me into the ditch," recalled Brett. "I lost control and didn't know if I was alive or dead."

Brett was hospitalized for two weeks with a concussion, cracked vertebra in his back, and a bruised liver, as well as severe bruises to his left arm and right side. Luckily for Brett, he was wearing his seat belt or his injuries would have been even more serious.

A week after he was released from the hospital, however, Brett was right back in for surgery to remove a section of his small intestine. "Thirty inches of my intestines dies in the crash, but it took awhile for it to contract. But once it did, no

61

food could pass through my system, and the pain was awful."

Although Brett was supposed to be out of action for five to six weeks following the surgery, he was back practicing in just two weeks, and two weeks after that played a key role in leading USM to a stunning 27–24 upset over Alabama in Birmingham. "You can call it a miracle or a legend or anything you want to," said Alabama coach Gene Stallings. "I just know on that day, Brett Favre was bigger than life."

For Brett, just getting back on to the field was a significant victory. "When I was in the hospital, there was a time when I didn't know whether I would ever get back and win a game like this, it really means a lot." And what made it even that much more satisfying was that the win had come against a major football power. "Southern Miss was a place where everyone had been rejected by the big schools. We were the Island of Misfits. But we thrived on that. We'd play Alabama, Auburn, and there'd be stories in the papers about how we'd been rejected by them. So when we came out and won a game against one of those teams, our guys would be yelling on the field, 'What's wrong with us now?' It was a great way to play."

Brett went on to lead USM to an 8–3 regular season record, and then closed out his career as a Golden Eagle in a blaze of glory by completing 28 of 39 passes, good for 341 yards and a pair of touchdowns, as Southern Miss knocked off North Carolina State in the All-American Bowl. After coming to the campus as the quarterback that no one really wanted, Brett left the school holding virtually every passing record in the USM record book.

4. A New Start

After the conclusion of his senior season at USM, Brett was invited to play in the Senior Bowl, one of the postseason college all-star games that serve to showcase talent for NFL teams. But Brett's performance in the Senior Bowl didn't do anything to raise his stock with the pro scouts. As Irvin Favre noted, "It was a sloppy day and Brett had a terrible game."

The all-star games aren't necessarily all that important to college All-Americans and players who come out of colleges with major football programs, but they can be important in either boosting or dampening the draft position or even, potentially, the career of someone like Brett, who comes out of a second-tier football school.

Fortunately for Brett, he became a last-minute replacement player in the East-West Shrine Game, an all-star game which features most of the best college seniors in the country. Brett put on such a razor-sharp performance in that star-studded contest that he not only raised his standing among NFL talent scouts in general, but also wound up impressing two people in particular, Mike Holmgren and Ron Wolf, who would play important roles in Brett's NFL future.

Holmgren at the time was the offensive coordinator of the San Francisco 49ers, while Wolf was the personnel director of the New York Jets. Wolf was so jazzed by Brett's performance in the Shrine game that he sold the Jets staff on the idea of making Brett the team's top pick in the upcoming NFL draft.

The Jets, who didn't have a first-round selection in the 1991 draft, were set to take Brett in the second round, which would have made him the 34th player to be chosen. "The Jets had Brett on the telephone before he was selected, and they said, 'We're going to take you with the next pick,'" recalled Irvin Favre. But while the Jets were on the phone, the Atlanta Falcons, who had the 33rd pick in the draft, snatched Brett out of their eager jaws.

Brett, who signed a three-year, $1.2 million contract with the Falcons, was delighted to have the opportunity to begin fulfilling his boyhood dreams, despite the fact that he went to training camp as the number four quarterback on Atlanta's depth chart.

Like all rookie signal callers, Brett had some trouble in learning a new system and an entirely new playbook, and for awhile he even had trouble throwing a spiral. "I've been tight and sort of stiff," Brett acknowledged at the time. "The thing is, when you take the snap and step back, it's not like reading a book. I mean, one time I'll stay with a receiver too long. The next time, I'll try to push a ball into an opening that maybe isn't do-able. I realize there are going to be bad days and good days. At this level, though, it just doesn't come easy."

What made the situation even more difficult for Brett, both physically and psychologically, was that the Falcons, under then-head coach Jerry Glanville, were one of the few NFL teams that operated out of the wide-open run-and-shoot offense. And as Brett noted, "I'm a drop-back passer, not a run-and-shoot guy."

Although Brett, temporarily and somewhat by default, became the No. 2 quarterback behind Chris Miller midway through training camp, the Falcons coaching staff decided that they didn't want to enter the regular season without an experienced backup. So they traded a future fifth-round draft choice to the San Diego Chargers for Billy Joe Tolliver to serve as Miller's understudy.

Brett was deeply discouraged by his demotion. "When you're third string and not taking any snaps in practice, it's like you're a nobody," declared Brett. But instead of rolling up his sleeves and working as hard as he could to develop his game, his body, and his football mind, Brett sulked and didn't put in the effort that was required to gain Glanville's confidence or to position himself for the following season. As Irvin Favre noted, "The number three guy gets virtually no reps during practice. That left Brett really depressed, and it wound up affecting his work habits."

His poor work habits also affected his playing time during the 1991 season, which consisted of cameo roles in two games and a stat line that read five passes, zero completions, and two interceptions. Brett's prospects weren't all that bright in Atlanta, but luckily for him, Ron Wolf had been hired as general manager of the Green Bay Packers. Wolf, remembering Brett's performance in the East-West Shrine Game, made the aquisition of the strong-armed quarterback a top priority, which he did with a deal that brought Brett to Green Bay in exchange for the Packers' No. 1 pick in the 1992 NFL draft.

Wolf took a lot of heat in Green Bay for trading away a No. 1 pick for a third stringer. "'Have you lost your mind?' was what most people wanted to know," recalled Wolf. "But I just really liked him. He has a toughness and a competitiveness that we like a lot, but the biggest attribute he possesses is leadership. He just has that unexplainable something."

Mike Holmgren, whom Wolf had hired as the team's new head coach, was also excited at the prospect of having Brett in a Packers uniform. "At Southern Mississippi, he showed a competitive instinct in bringing his team from behind in dramatic fashion to beat Alabama and Auburn — two teams that were a lot better than USM. That told me that he's got the right stuff."

The right stuff is exactly what Wolf and Holmgren were trying to bring back to Green Bay, a long-floundering franchise that had for a time been the best in the league. Under legendary coach Vince Lombardi, the person for whom the Super Bowl trophy is named, the Packers had won three NFL titles between 1961 and 1965, and then had gone on to smashing victories in Super Bowl I in 1966 and Super Bowl II in 1967. Those Packer teams were so dominant that no less than ten of their players have earned a place in the Pro Football Hall of Fame, while the city of Green Bay came to be known as Title Town USA.

In the 24 years between 1968 and 1991, however, the Packers had been able to post only four winning seasons. Wolf and Holmgren were determined to reverse the team's decline, and they expected Brett to become a cornerstone of Green Bay's return to its former greatness.

Brett received news of the trade while he was eating a meal back home in Kiln. "I really didn't know what to think at first. But then Ron called and said, 'We're excited to have you. We gave up a first round pick for you, and we feel like in a couple of years you can be our starter,' I felt really good that somebody believed in me again. It was like turning over a new leaf in my career."

Brett also welcomed the opportunity to play for Holmgren, a coach that he had first met at the Shrine Game and then later that spring, when Holmgren had gone to USM to workout Brett prior to the 1991 draft. "We sat up in the stands for about 30 minutes afterwards and he just seemed like a great guy," explained Brett. "'He told me, 'Look, I don't foresee us drafting a quarterback'" — which was not surprising, since Holmgren had still been with the 49ers at the time, a team that already had three quarterbacks, namely Joe Montana, Steve Young, and Steve Bono —"'but I really like you.'"

Brett was totally upbeat about the trade and ready to go to Green Bay and get his career back on track. "I have a lot to learn, not only about this offense, but about the NFL. But I'm a big guy with a strong arm. I'm an intelligent guy when it comes to football, and I'm a competitor." In fact, the only memories that he was interested in carrying with him from Atlanta were the good times that he had shared with his teammates, including Deion Sanders, who had given Brett the nickname of "Country."

Brett also showed his enthusiasm for Green Bay by immediately agreeing to become the Wisconsin spokesperson for the Punt, Pass, and Kick competition. "I grew up in the organization, so it was a natural thing for me to do," Brett said. "We bring all of the kids in for halftime of one of our games during the season to compete and I always go and talk to them before the game. It's something I still do."

Irvin Favre, meanwhile, assured the people of Green Bay that his son was the real article. "The fans there want to win badly and so does Brett. He's a battler. If he's got the football in his hands and you're looking for something impossible, Brett can do it."

With two young veterans, Don Majkowski and Mike Tomzcak, on the roster, no one on the Packers staff actually expected the ball to be in Brett's hands too often during the 1992 season. In fact, very few first-or second-year quarterbacks even get to start an NFL game, except in an emergency. Coaches prefer to bring young signal callers along slowly, allowing them to gradually absorb the increasingly complicated offenses and ever-changing defenses.

Although Brett was extremely short on NFL experience, he was overflowing with confidence. "I really feel like I'm going to play a lot of this year, and I think that everybody else does, too," said Brett at his first Packers training camp. "The toughest part is becoming a starting quarterback. Once I'm in, it's going to be over," said Brett, referring to the competition. "I really believe it. Just like college."

5. A Storybook Kind of Season

Brett's comments seemed like so much training camp boasting as he started the season firmly anchored to Green Bay's bench, while the Packers dropped their season opener at Lambeau Field to the visiting Minnesota Vikings. But after Majkowski failed to get the offense revved in the first half of the Packers' next game versus the Tampa Bay Bucaneers, Holmgren pulled the plug on him and sent Brett in to try his hand in the second half.

The results of Brett's first sustained NFL action were inconclusive. He connected on 8 of 14 passes for 73 yards, suffering one interception and four sacks while Green Bay bit the dust 31–3. So Brett was back on the bench the following week as the 2–0 Bengals visited Lambeau field. But during the Packers' second offensive series, Majkowski suffered strained ligaments in his left ankle, so Brett was rushed back into action and took the team on a wild roller-coaster ride that alternated between absolutely awesome and slapstick comedy.

"I saw things on the football field I didn't even know we had in our offense," said Holmgren. "He was running around so much, I barely recognized anything."

Nobody had to tell Brett, who fumbled four times, was sacked five times, and had a number of potential interceptions bobbled by defenders, that he had some problems out on the field. "I made enough mistakes in that first half to last a whole year. I was wondering if they were going to run me out of town."

But in the second half, and especially on the Packers' final two possessions, Brett was magnificent. On the first possession, with Green Bay trailing 23–10 and only eight minutes left on the clock, Brett led the Packers on an 88–yard drive that narrowed the gap to 23–17. Then, with only 54 seconds and no time-outs left, Brett took the Packers from their own 8-yard line to the Bengals 35-yard line before he drilled a touchdown pass that tied the game at 23.

Brett was so excited that he ran around the filed high-fiving every teammate he could find, and almost forgot to take the snap for the point-after attempt that gave the Pack the breathtaking 24–23 victory.

After the game Brett admitted that at times, "I was shaking," but he managed to shield his nervousness from his teammates and project an air of confidence and competence. "He was very clear with his calls," said center James Camper. "I think he kept getting more relaxed as the game went on."

"It was weird," said Brett. "They backed up and played a two-deep zone on us at the end. They blitzed us early and got to us. Then they went to a two-deep zone and we just gashed them. Thank goodness. If they'd have blitzed us, they had us. Back then, we didn't know what we were doing when they blitzed.

"'I don't know how we won as bad as I played that day. Once in a while, I'll look at that film and go, 'Aww! I was awful. Awful lucky.'"

There might have been an element of luck in Brett's wildwest show, but Ron Lynn, the Bengals defensive coordinator, saw a lot of John Elway, the comeback king of the Denver Broncos, in Brett's performance. "For 10 series we had pretty much kicked him around, and then he brought them back in those last two series," Lynn said. "I can vividly see most of those plays. He had a little Elway to him in that the game wasn't over until the gun was shot.

"I don't think he has John's escape ability, but he had that kind of confidence. There's a little but of gunslinger-type attitude: 'I'll take my best shots and you might beat me, but I'll be back tomorrow.' You like that in a quarterback."

Green Bay's quarterback coach at the time, Steve Mariucci who is now the head coach of the University of California at Berkeley, also thought that he had seen the future. "It was an indicator of what's to come." Meanwhile, back in Kiln, Irvin

Favre was filled with pride as he offered a friendly warning to NFL defenses, "When Brett has the ball in his hand, don't ever turn your back on him, because he'll beat you."

Although there would be some bumps in the road, and some moments of doubt and anguish by both Brett and the coaching staff, Brett did become the starter in the next game and has been in that role ever since.

Despite many people believing that Brett might turn into a pumpkin in his following outing, he played under control and helped lead the Packers to a second straight win, 17–3, over the previously unbeaten Pittsburgh Steelers. While the Green Bay defense was throwing a steel curtain around the Steelers defense, Brett was connecting on 14 of 19 pass attempts, including a 76-yarder to Sterling Sharpe, his All-Pro wide receiver.

By a quirk of the schedule, the Packers' next game was in Atlanta, and although Brett tried to play down the revenge factor, everybody knew that he would have loved to ground the Falcons. But despite completing 33 of 43 pass attempts for 276 yards and a TD, Brett also threw a pair of interceptions as the Falcons soared to a 24–10 win.

The loss to Atlanta was the first in a three-game losing streak that saw the Packers outscored by a total of 71 to 26. The problem wasn't in the passing game, where Brett and Sterling Sharpe—who wound up setting what was then the single-season reception record with 108 catches—were shining. The problem was instead traceable to an ineffective offensive line and a pitiful running game, which ranked only 20th in the NFL in yardage gained, and which was particularly inept at punching the ball into the end zone from anywhere inside the opponents' 20-yard line.

None the less, the lack of scoring caused Holmgren to publicly muse about switching back to Majkowski, which caused Brett to have a few fretful days. But Holmgren ultimately gave the nod to Brett, who responded by throwing a pair of TD passes against the Detroit Lions, which helped the Packers out of their slump and into a 27–13 win at the Silverdome. But only one week later, Brett showed the inconsistently which is a hallmark of an inexperienced quarterback by throwing a trio of interceptions in Green Bay's 27–7 road loss to the New York Giants.

With their record down to 3–6, it seemed as if the Packers were sinking toward their third straight losing season as they prepared to host the playoff-bound Philadelphia Eagles. But instead of laying down and absorbing another loss, the Packers rose up and defeated the high-flying Eagles. The game proved to be a pivotal point in the Packers' season, as well as in their long-range goal of becoming one of the elite teams in the NFL. And the win served as a bright and defining moment in Brett's brief career.

Early on, the game actually took on a darkish tint when the Eagles' All-Pro defensive end, Reggie White, slammed Brett to the ground with such force that Brett suffered a separated left shoulder. Almost miraculously, perhaps foolishly, Brett stayed in the game despite pain that was so throbbing that he couldn't even turn towards his left to deliver a handoff.

"I know when I got hurt, there was no way I was coming out. The doctor looked at my shoulder and it was really swollen. There was a big knot where the separation was. Coach Mike Holmgren wanted to lift me. I said, "No way. I've put too much into this game. I'm not coming out."

At halftime, as the marching band blared and the cheerleaders pranced around while fans lined up at the refreshment stands, as usual, Brett was in the Green Bay locker room, having a painkiller shot into his shoulder so that he could go out and play the gladiator for the second half. "I was determined to finish what I started," declared Brett, who did just that, as well as throw a pair of touchdown passes that led the Packers to a 27–24 come-from-behind upset victory. "When we won that

71

game, I knew I could play with the big guys," recalled Brett.

The win propelled the Packers to a six-game winning streak, the first time since 1965 that Green Bay had experienced such a long stretch of "Ws." "I don't know if Brett realizes what he's doing," said Packer safety Chuck Cecil. "He's just an old country boy doing the best he can, and it turns out the best he can is a lot better that a lot of people thought he could do."

Only a streak-breaking, season-ending loss to the Vikings prevented the 9–7 Packers from charging into the playoff picture. But even that disappointing loss couldn't dim the luster from the team's spectacular turnaround or the high wattage performance that earned Brett an invitation to play in the Pro Bowl, the NFL's postseason all-star game.

Brett, at 23 years, 3 months and 28 days, was, at the time, the youngest quarterback to play in a Pro Bowl. He was thrilled at the opportunity to mingle with the likes of Troy Aikman, Steve Young, and Barry Sanders, and surprised when they said hello to him. "I'm thinking, 'How do they know who I am?'" Brett was also delighted to leave behind the subfreezing weather in Green Bay to play a game in balmy Hawaii. "I'm having a blast," crowed Brett. "Is this great or what?"

It had been a storybook kind of season for Brett, who had gone from being a bench warmer to Pro Bowl performer, while breaking the Packers' single-season record for passing percentage, which had been set by Bart Starr, the Hall of Fame quarterback from the great Green Bay teams of the 1960s.

Brett, though, was already looking beyond the clear blue skies of Hawaii. "I'm the youngest guy here, which is quite an accomplishment," he said. "But I don't want to just be a one-year phenomenon."

If Brett needed any prodding to keep on working and learning, Mike Holmgren was always there to supply the helpful push. "He is not nearly as good as he can be and will be if he continues to work hard. He can't lose sight of the fact that he got where he is because he's worked hard. Consistency in performance is the key, and I'll do everything that I can to prevent him from being a one-year wonder. But I don't think he'll succumb to that. He's got the right temperament; he wants to do well. He's got everything it takes."

6. Great Expectations

Brett's performance in 1992 served as the catalyst for a lot of offseason changes, including the release of Don Majkowski. "I told Brett that this was his team," recalled Holmgren. "I told him to take it from there." Brett's play had also acted as a lure for Reggie White, who was the most pursued prize in 1993's free-agent bazaar. When White, generally considered to be the top defensive end of his era, was asked why he had selected Green Bay, he cited Brett's emergence as a key factor. "Brett has all the qualities of a championship quarterback," explained White, who had set his sights on a Super Bowl ring.

Brett appreciated the praise, but he was smart enough to know that he had to prove himself on the field again, or fall back and become just another flash in the pan like Majkowski, who had continually pulled rabbits out of his hat while leading the Packers to a 10-win season in 1989. "I hope I'm not a one-year wonder," said Brett, expressing some doubt about his ability to duplicate the spectacular success he had achieved a year earlier. Brett also felt slightly cowed by the unreasonable level of excitement that was being generated by the media and the long-suffering fans in Green Bay. "People are putting a lot of expectations on us, picking us to win the division and go to the Super Bowl, and that could become a burden," said Brett, who also had to contend with a coaching staff that had made a commitment to him, and expected Brett to work hard at honing his physical skills and improving his on-field decision making.

Brett had enjoyed relatively clean sailing throughout the previous season when expectations had been meager and every accomplishment had been an unexpected plus. But those same accomplishments had created great expectations in 1993 and helped turn the season into a long and rocky road.

Brett got a taste of what lay ahead when, after he had led the

Packers to a 36–6 opening-day route over the L.A. Rams, Holmgren took him to task for his careless flings, including one on which the ball bounced off two Rams defenders before settling into Sharpe's hands for a 50-yard score, one of Brett's two TD tosses of the day. "That wasn't a pass, it was a launch," Holmgren said in an irritable tone that indicated that he considered himself to be a football coach and not a NASA flight controller.

At first, Brett acted defensively to Holmgren's criticism, but then he quickly reversed himself and conceded that the coach had the right approach. "I realize I need to be more disciplined to get to the next level. I want to build on last year and eventually lead this team to a Super Bowl. Coach knows what it takes because he's been there with the 49ers."

By the season's midpoint, however, the team of high hopes was floundering along with a 4–4 record, while Brett was leading the league in interceptions thrown and hearing about it from disappointed fans and media people. "I'd be lying here if I sat here and said I was playing well, because I'm not," admitted Brett, who too often tried to force a pass in situations where it would have been wiser to take a sack or throw the ball away. "That's probably one of my toughest things to deal with, especially after I've made a bad play. The next play I feel like I have to put up a score."

The Packers coaching staff, who knew that Brett was making progress and also realized that he was once again playing under the handicap of not having a credible running attack to ease the pressure on the passing game, was quick to respond to Brett's critics.

"He's a better player," Holmgren said. "I don't know how many times I have to say that. He's a better player now than he was last year. At times errors will take place because of his inexperience. Any time you have a young quarterback that's your starting quarterback, those things are going to happen."

Brett was working through the normal growing pains of learning to play what is arguably the most difficult position in any team sport. Playing quarterback in the NFL isn't as simple as it seems from the stands or from watching it on TV. It's not just a question of calling a play, taking the snap from the center, and then handing off or throwing the ball. A quarterback first has to learn an entire new code language so that he can call the proper play and the proper formation from which it should be run. The same exact play can be run from different formations, and players will have different assignments to carry out depending upon the play selection and the formation from which it is run. The quarterback also has to know what each of his ten teammates is supposed to do on each play and in each formation. And he also has to remember what the snap count is, and to keep changing it so that the defense can't time its charge.

In addition to knowing the code names of all the plays and formations and the roles of everyone on his own team, the quarterback has to be able to come up to the line of scrimmage, take a second or two to scan the defense, and recognize what formation the defense is in—are they, for example, playing zone or man-to-man in the backfield? Are they double-covering any receiver? Who has drawn single coverage? Is a linebacker or two going to blitz? Are they more vulnerable to a pass or a running play?—and then process the information through his brain like a high-speed computer. Then, he has to decide whether to stay with the play that was called because it should work against the defense he's looking at, or to change the play by calling an audible—an entirely different play or formation called out to his team at the line of scrimmage—because the play that was called won't work against the defensive formation that he sees. The quarterback has to see and decide all this in seconds, and he has to know the plays and formations and assignments so well that he can do it as automatically as crossing the street when the light turns green.

John Hadl, a former All-Pro quarterback, perfectly captured the sense of panic that a young quarterback feels when all the players are moving, but he can't decipher the patterns. "Things happen so fast out there, it's like a jailbreak. You have to learn the system and the way the coaches want to have it done. Then you start to think quite a bit, and sometimes you think too much. Then you go blank."

Brett started the second half of the season on a high note by collaborating with Sharpe on a 54-yard pass with under a minute to play that set up a game-winning field goal against the Saints in the Superdome. Although a last minute win always feels good, Brett was especially happy to pull off such a dramatic play in front of a large contingent of his fans who had driven down from Kiln, and to do it on the same field where Archie Manning, one of his boyhood heroes, had performed.

The victory was the start of a three-game streak that continued with a straightforward win over the Lions and a down-to-the-wire nail-biter against Tampa Bay in which Brett led the Packers on a 15-play, 75-yards scoring drive capped by his game-winning scoring strike to Sterling Sharpe.

On the play prior to the touchdown pass, Brett had taken a stiff blow to his left thigh, so instead of celebrating the big win Brett spent a sleepless night in a brace that locked his leg in place so that his quadricep muscle was kept stretched instead of being allowed to tighten. "The heel of my foot was nearly touching my buttocks, it was pulled back so far," said Brett. But with Green Bay tied with the Lions for first place in the NFC Central Division, Brett was more concerned about the upcoming game with the Bears than he was for his own comfort. "The bottom line is, we have to win this game, and we can't worry about bodily parts."

Brett recovered in time to sting the Bears secondary for a pair of touchdowns and a career-high 402 yards passing, but he also fumbled once and threw three interceptions, and the team from the Windy City converted three of those miscues into 21 points on their way to a 30–17 win.

Green Bay rebounded to take two of its next three games to up their record to 9–6. But in the season finale showdown against the Lions, with the division title and home field advantage in the playoffs riding on the outcome, Brett was picked off four times as the Pack lost the game and everything that went with it.

Those that knew him best, like his former college coach, Curly Hallman, were confident that Brett would bounce back. "Let me tell you about Brett Favre. He might be struggling a bit now, but he will survive in the NFL. In two or three years, he'll be the best QB in the NFL. Someday they'll have another championship in Green Bay, and Brett Favre will help them get it."

The following week, the Packers were back in the Silverdome and once against trailed their hosts, 24–21, thanks in part to a third-quarter pick of a Brett pass that was returned for a 15-yard touchdown. But with less than a minute left to play, Brett took a snap just inside the midfield stripe. While Brett rolled to his left to avoid the Detroit pass rush, Sterling Sharpe was streaking down the right sideline, seemingly out of possible passing range.

Brett, in fact, didn't even look at Sharpe, but instead drew a bead on tight end Ed West who, like Brett, was moving diagonally across the field from right to left. After a short, safe pass competition to West, there would still be time to go for the win or a score-tying field goal which would send the game into overtime.

But suddenly, Brett pulled his arm down as a familiar and sometimes frightening thought hot-wired through his brain: "There must be something better." Brett glanced right, saw Sharpe racing for the end zone and in one fluid, whiplike motion re-cocked his arm and delivered a perfect though implausible game-winning pass to Sharpe, their third scoring collaboration of the day. "I was so excited that I started hyperventilating," said Brett.

Ironically, the spectacular across-the-body pass was a

prime example of the type of play that caused the Packers coaching staff to cringe. Although Brett was a gifted improviser who could sometimes turn broken plays and forced throws into breathtaking results, it was a facet of his game that more often produced heartache as well as being a key contributor in his NFL-high 24 interceptions. "That's my problem," agreed Brett. "Sometimes there's not something better."

The following week the Packers' playoff run came to a stop in Dallas where they were defeated 27-17 by a Cowboys team that was on its way to a second consecutive Super Bowl win. Although Brett passed for a pair of scores while racking up 331 passing yards, one shy of the team's single-game playoff record, he also threw two more interceptions against the Cowboys.

Despite having led Green Bay to its first full season playoff appearance since 1972, it had been a trying and testing period for Brett, who saw his year-to-year interception number soar while his quarterback rating dropped like a stone from 85.3 to 72.2. "It was a tough year for me," said Brett, thinking not just about the numbers, but the criticism and the pressure of being squeezed in a vice by the pressure of great expectations. "But it really helped me. In order to get to the top you have to scrape the bottom of the barrel first. I definitely did that, But I learned a lot from it, too."

7. Going for Perfect

After an offseason spent as a gym rat, Brett reported to training camp in the finest shape he'd ever been in. He also felt good about his new five-year, $19 million dollar contract, and was just raring to get started. But almost before Brett had a chance to say hello, Mike Holmgren hit him between the eyes by announcing that Brett was, in effect, on trial. "This is the pivotal year for Brett," declared Holmgren, adding that he wouldn't hesitate to bench his quarterback if Brett didn't control his carelessness with the football.

It wasn't clear whether Holmgren actually meant what he said, or was simply trying to scare Brett into cutting down on his interceptions. Whatever the reality was, Brett seemed stunned by Holmgren's stance. "I don't know what to believe," said Brett. "He knows I'm going to make mistakes, I get sacked, I fumble and I throw interceptions, but he also knows I'm going to win ball games for him. I may run around like a chicken without a head, but I'm going to win."

The problem, though, was that Brett's recklessness also lost games. Quarterback coach Steve Mariucci, always a strong supporter of Brett, explained that the coaches realized that some interceptions were an integral part of the game. "But Brett has to stop the ones where he gets pulled to the ground or a guy is hanging on his leg and he just wings it up there with a hope and a prayer. He has enough wherewithal and poise to say, 'All right, they won this one. I'll eat it.'"

Brett, however, started the 1994 season by playing with the same reckless abandon that in the past had produced brilliant moments, but uneven results. With the team at 1–2, Brett persuaded Holmgren that part of the problem was that they never discussed upcoming games. "We never really communicated during the week about which plays we would be using. Then Sunday comes and he would call the plays and I would just run them."

Brett's strategy seemed to have an immediate payoff as he completed 30-of-39 passes for 306 yards, 3 TDs and zero interceptions, while the Packers trounced Tampa Bay, 30–3. "That's probably as comfortable as I've ever felt here," said Brett after the game. "We communicated a lot on the sidelines, with Mike telling me what he's be calling on the next drive. That helped me a lot."

The results appeared to be short-lived, though, because Brett was picked off twice in the next game, a losing effort against the New England Patriots, and then struggled through a miserable first half against the Rams, which provoked a steady stream of boos at Lambeau Field. "I'm sure teammates wanted to boo me too," joked Brett after he had turned in a gritty second-half performance that rallied the Packers to a 24–17 win. But there were no jokes the following week. After throwing an interception that set up the Vikings' only TD, Brett suffered a first-quarter hip injury and for the first time in his NFL career, was unable to finish a game.

On the plane ride home from Minnesota, Brett mulled over the Packers 3–4 record as well as his own inconsistency, and wound up making a commitment to himself. "I decided, enough of this already. From now on I'm going to be the best quarterback in the NFL." Brett, though, was uncertain if he'd get the chance to live up his words. "I thought if I had one more bad game, I was gone."

Holmgren, sensing the vulnerability that Brett was feeling, called a meeting and told Brett to relax. "I told him, 'You're my guy. You and I are joined at the hip. Either we go to the top of the mountain together, or we're both going to wind up in the dumpster.'"

Armed with that vote of confidence and his own determination, Brett began delivering the goods the very next week by leading the Packers over the Bears 33–6 on Halloween night.

The extraordinary aspect of the game, which was played in a cold, cyclonic rainstorm, was that Brett; who passed for one TD and scrambled 36-yards for another one, threw only 15 passes and didn't commit a single turnover, while playing under absolute self-control. "That was one of the best games I've played in three years," said a maturing Brett about his accomplishments in a game which stood in stark contrast to the Packers' previous losing effort at Soldiers Field, in which Brett threw for over 400 yards and five TDs but also turned the ball over five times. "But I can play better."

Then Brett went and burned up the league by throwing for 24 touchdowns and only seven interceptions while leading Green Bay to six wins in its final nine games, raising the team's record to 9–7. Brett capped off his pivotal season by piloting the Packers to a playoff-clinching win in Tampa Bay, connecting with Sterling Sharpe on a trio of TD tosses that raised Brett's total to an NFL-best 33. "Now I feel good, not just physically, but mentally. I feel like I really am one of the best quarterbacks in the league," said Brett, who was also quick to praise his receivers, the improved offensive line, and the coaching staff that had stuck with him though the tough times.

"I need to keep saying things to remind myself, 'On this play, it might not be open, so what are you going to do if it's not?'" said Brett, who had the second highest quarterback rating in the league. "It's not easy, but that's what separates the best ones from the average ones. I think I'm heading in the right direction. I'm doing a lot better this year in [those] situations. That's the most important thing."

Then, for the second successive year, Brett guided the Packers to a wild-card win over the Lions before being bumped out of the playoffs in Dallas. This time, though, Brett wasn't looking back and singing the blues as he had the previous year. This time around he was enjoying his success and looking towards the future. "I've always made a lot of mistakes and will probably continue to make more until I quit playing. But I would assume that year after year I'll continue to get better."

• • • • • •

Throughout their first three years together in Green Bay, Holmgren had been prodding Brett to reach for the perfect game. Holmgren knew from coaching Joe Montana, who is generally conceded to be the greatest quarterback of all time, that if a quarterback has the physical tools and mental toughness to do the job, as Brett does, then the only other elements needed to achieve a perfect game were the drive and discipline to go after it.

Holmgren also reasoned that once Brett had experienced the ecstatic feeling of a perfect game, he would strive to recapture that feeling in every game he played.

Brett, however, had always expressed resistance to the idea that he could play that perfect game, seeming to accept his erratic play as being of a piece with him and beyond the possibility of elimination. "It sometimes seems like Mike is waiting for the day when I step out of my shell and suddenly I'm a perfect quarterback," Brett had said during the 1994 summer camp. But that will never happen, and he knows it. He knows that I'll never play a perfect game."

So it was ironic that only a year after he had derided the possibility of his playing a single perfect game, that Brett would come close to playing a completely perfect season.

In the first half of the season, Brett, simply picking up the pace that he had set at the end of the 1994 campaign, had already passed for 17 TDs and run for two more, which gave him a big hand in 19 of Green Bay's 21 offensive touchdowns. But after the ninth game of the season, a loss to the Vikings in which he was forced out with an ankle injury, Brett turned the throttle full blast and reached an entirely different level of play.

During that spectacular seven-game stretch which he began by passing for five TDs in a win over the Bears while hobbling on his injured ankle, Brett completed 70.3 percent of his passes and threw for 21 TDs and only two interceptions while compiling an off-the-charts quarterback rating of 123.0. Over the course of the full season, Brett wound up leading the NFL in passing yards and threw an NFC-record 38 touchdown passes, the third highest single-season total in league history.

Moreover, his performance carried the 11–5 Packers—who set an NFL record for fewest turnovers in a season, 16—to their first division title since 1972, while earning him a roomful of plaques and trophies as well as a trip to the Pro Bowl as the NFC's staring quarterback. "He does everything you can ask from a quarterback, and he's still young and learning," glowed Mike Holmgren.

Then Brett put on a commanding performance, in which he threw for a trio of TDs and no interceptions, while leading the Packers over the Falcons, 37–20, in the opening round of the playoffs. The following week, Brett scorched the 49ers for a pair of scoring passes while piloting the Packers past the defending Super Bowl champions, 27–17. "I'm not going to lie to you, I'm happy with how I played," said Brett, who played errorless football against the NFL's top-rated defense while outdueling San Francisco quarterback Steve Young. "Beating the 49ers was about the biggest win I've ever had."

Brett's performance earned high praise from Bill Walsh, a 49ers executive who had coached the team to three Super Bowl wins. "He's outstanding," raved Walsh. "I'm almost surprised at how well he's developed. He's been good from the start, but he has full command of the offense now. He has that command of the game like Montana did. It's really something to appreciate."

That victory earned the Packers a ticket to Dallas, where they squared off against the Cowboys for the NFC championship, Green Bay's first title matchup since 1967.

Brett was obviously edgy early in the game, going 0–6 while having a screen pass picked off by Dallas tackle Leon

Lett, setting up a score which put the home team ahead 14–3. Brett eventually settled down, however, and began putting on a masterful performance, including a pair of TD passes that helped propel the Packers to a 24–17 halftime lead. Although the Cowboys leapfrogged past the Packers, 31–27, on a fourth-quarter run by Emmitt Smith, Brett had the Packers driving and threatening to retake the lead later in the quarter. But then disaster struck when Cowboys cornerback Larry Brown picked off one of Brett's passes deep in Dallas territory and returned it to their 48-yard line. The Cowboys, who went on to win their third NFL title in four years by beating the Steelers soundly in Super Bowl XXX, quickly converted the turnover into another score that put the game out of reach at 38–27. "If I don't throw that interception, we win the game," said Brett, who finished the day with 303 yards passing and a trio of TD passes. "If we had scored on that possession, I think it would have put a stake through their hearts. Unfortunately, it didn't happen like that, but we did come a long way."

Brett had also come a long way, from a high school quarter-back nobody wanted to the top rung of NFL signal callers. "I've always expected great things of myself," said Brett, in a matter-of-fact tone. "It comes from my parents. It comes from the environment I grew up in. Things never came easy for us, but I always had a feeling things would work out."

Things worked out so well that Brett made a virtual sweep of the major awards for the 1995 season including the Sporting News Player of the Year, which is voted on by the NFL person-nel directors. Brett was also named the league's All-Pro quarterback and the NFL's MVP in balloting conducted by members of the Associated Press. "It's hard to even explain how much that means to me," said Brett. "When you think about all the great players you play with and against, it's just overwhelming."

Brett, though, left no doubt about what his ultimate goal

was. "The individual honors are nice, but I know that winning Super Bowls is how great quarterbacks are measured. It would mean everything to me to bring the Packers back to the Super Bowl, there's no doubt that before my career's over, I'm going to win a Super Bowl in Green Bay. That's what I'm living for."

And then he left a scary message for opposing defenses to consider during the offseason. "I can do better in every phase of the game."

Epilogue

Football fans were stunned when on May 14, 1996 Brett held a press conference to announce that he had been in counseling for addiction to painkillers and that he was about to take the next step and enter a clinic to deal with that addiction.

The only people who weren't shocked were the people closest to him, such as Steve Mariucci. The former quarterback coach apparently realized during the 1995 season that Brett's use of Vicodin might be out of control and informed the Packers training staff of his concern.

Apparently, however, the supply of Vicodin was limitless, available not only from the team trainers but from private doctors and even teammates who no longer had need of their prescribed pills. Deanna Tynes, Brett's long-time girlfriend who lives with him and their daughter, has reported that she would find pills all over the house.

Tynes also reported that Brett would regularly sit stupor-like in front of the television into the early hours of the morning, unable to fall asleep. Tynes tried to get Brett to seek help, but in his narrow field of vision there was no problem. "I'm in the best shape of my life," he is said to have told Tynes. "Why should I stop what's helping me through this?"

The answer came on February 27, 1996, while Brett was lying in a hospital bed, recovering from surgery to the ankle that he injured in October 1995 in a game against the Vikings. Suddenly, Brett fell unconscious. When he awoke, John Gray, a Green Bay team doctor told Brett that he had suffered a life-threatening seizure that could have been brought on by Brett's heavy use of Vicodin.

At that moment, Brett decided to stop taking all painkillers and voluntarily entered the NFL's substance abuse program. With those two decisive steps, Brett began to dig himself out of the ditch that he had apparently been digging since 1990, when he first began taking painkillers as an aftermath of his automobile accident.

"I'm not blaming anyone," said Brett at the news conference, standing up and taking the hit the way he always prided himself on doing on the football field.

The reality, though, is that there is, like with many problems, plenty of blame to spread around. While Brett is ultimately responsible for his actions, his addiction was, like football, a team game. As Robert Huizenga, a former team doctor of the Oakland Raiders and a past president of the NFL Physician's Society, put the matter, "This is not an isolated incident. We want people to play hurt, and when someone doesn't play hurt, he's no longer our hero. We need a system where a physician, without fear of losing his job, can say to an athlete, 'The injury is not healed. You cannot play.'"

That system is certainly not in place now, and physicians do have families feed, too, but one can't help but wondering when the Hippocratic Oath that doctors are required to take was superseded by pro sport's unwritten code that the "show must go on."

The system that is in place does not subscribe, even in lip service, to the supposed ideal of a strong mind in a strong body. That certainly doesn't appear to be the goal of most major sports teams, which seem to treat athletes as disposable objects. The primary objective for both teams and players apparently is to win, gain recognition, and make piles of money. So the ideal of a strong mind in a healthy body has become grotesquely distorted into a warped reality of numbing the players' pain and sacrificing their bodies for dollars. Meanwhile the owners, most of whom have never taken a hit or dished one out, sit in their climate-controlled luxury boxes, drinking and socializing with their high-income guests, so far removed from the actual game that they have to view it on the TV monitors. And all the while the mantra, "Money, money, money, win, win, win at any cost" blazes continually like some sort of crazed anthem.

As Brett himself phrased the situation, "I'm 26 years old. I just threw 38 TD passes and I'm the NFL MVP. People look at me and think they'd love to be me. But if they knew what it took me to get where I am they wouldn't love to be me, I guarantee that. I'm entering a treatment center tomorrow. Would they love that?" queried Brett rhetorically, feeling like a failure to himself, his family and his teammates.

So when we look at Brett's streak of starting 62 games, the longest such streak among active quarterbacks, we should begin to look at it not just as a sign of grittiness—which it is—but also as a sign of human frailty, a fear of being replaced, and sadly enough, of having time pass you by.

Dear Reader,

One of the nicest rewards of being an author is receiving some very wonderful letters from readers. And while I don't want to discourage any writers, I thought I would use this page to answer the most asked questions that come in the mail.

I was born on November 14, 1941 in Brooklyn, which is one of the five boroughs that comprise New York City. I grew up on Ocean Parkway, and I spent most of the time through my teenage years playing one sport or another. In looking back, I wish I had spent some of that time reading some of the wonderful books that I later discovered by reading them with my children.

I'm not exactly sure why I became a writer, but I know that part of the reason is that I have a passion to communicate and create-whether I'm writing a book, baking a loaf of bread, or growing a flower or a broccoli. I've always enjoyed working with my hands, bringing something into life and sharing my ideas and feelings with other people.

I'm sure that another reason has to do with four wonderful teachers that I was fortunate enough to have when I was growing up. The first was my mother, Betty, who taught me the joy of music and to take life's bumps with a smile (she did it better than I do it) and to keep moving forward. She also taught me, as Martin Luther King, Jr., would try to teach the world, to judge people by the contents of their characters and their deeds, and not by the superficialities of skin color, their current or past country of origin, or their religious beliefs (or their lack of those beliefs.)

Then there was Katherine Lynch-a teacher of history and so much more-whose path I was so lucky to cross when I decided to spend my 10th grade in Silver Spring, Maryland. After all these years I still can't express just how much she gave me. Then came Malcolm Largman, my 11th grade English teacher at Lafayette High School, the first person to give me the notion and the confidence that I could become a writer.

Finally, there was Jackie Robinson, a great baseball player and phenomenal human being whose example taught me how to walk alone when I had to, and to confront ignorance and bigotry not with physical weapons or hatred, but with courage and dignity.

To all my teachers-past, present, and future-thank you!

Richard J. Brenner

If you want to write to the author, address your letter to:

> Richard J. Brenner
> c/o East End Publishing
> 54 Alexander Dr.
> Syosset NY 11791

Please note that letters *will not* be answered unless they include a self-addressed stamped envelope.

If you want to write to the players, address your letters to:

Deion Sanders
c/o Dallas Cowboys
One Cowboys Parkway
Irving TX 75063-4727

Brett Favre
c/o Green Bay Packers
P.O. Box 10628
Green Bay WI 54307-0628

Here are some other addresses:

Major League Baseball
350 Park Ave.
New York, N.Y. 10022

Mr. Paul Tagliabue
c/o NFL
410 Park Avenue
New York, N.Y. 10022

Sources

Appleton Post— Crescent

Football Digest

Green Bay Press— Gazette

Hattiesburg American

Aaron Klein, *Deion Sanders,* Walker and Co.

Milwaukee Journal

Milwaukee Sentinel

The New York Times

Jeff Savage, *Deion Sanders Star Athlete,*
  Emslow Publishers, Inc.

Sport

Sports Illustrated

Sports Illustrated for Kids

Stew Thornley, *Deion Sanders Prime Time Player,*
  Lerner Publications Co.

USA Today Baseball Weekly

DEION SANDERS

COLLEGE STATS

Football

Year	Interceptions	No.	Punt Returns Yards	Avg.	Touchdowns	Longest
1985	1	30	255	8.5	1	58
1986	4	31	290	9.4	0	32
1987	4	32	381	11.9	1	53
1988	5	33	503	15.2	1	76
Totals	14	126	1,429	7.3	3	76

Baseball

Year	Games	At-Bats	Runs	Hits	Avg.	Home Runs	RBI	Stolen Bases
1986	16	60	21	20	.333	1	14	11
1987	60	210	41	56	.267	3	21	27
Totals	76	270	62	76	.281	4	35	38

College World Series

Year	Games	At-Bats	Runs	Hits	Avg.	Home Runs	RBI	Stolen Bases
1987	3	11	0	3	.273	0	0	1

REGULAR SEASON BASEBALL STATS

Year	Club	AVG.	G	AB	R	H	2B	3B	HR	RBI	BB	SO	SB
1988	Sarasota	.280	17	75	7	21	4	2	0	6	2	10	11
	Ft. Lauderdale	.429	6	21	5	9	2	0	0	2	1	3	2
	Columbus	.150	5	20	3	3	1	0	0	0	1	4	1
1989	Albany	.286	33	119	28	34	2	2	1	6	11	20	17
	Columus	.278	70	259	38	72	12	7	5	30	22	46	16
	NEW YORK (AL)	.234	14	47	7	11	2	0	2	7	3	8	1
1990	Columbus	.321	22	84	21	27	7	1	2	10	17	15	9
	NEW YORK (AL)	.158	57	133	24	21	2	2	3	9	13	27	8
1991	Richmond	.262	29	130	20	34	6	3	5	16	10	28	12
	ATLANTA (NL)	.191	54	110	16	21	1	2	4	13	12	23	11
1992	ATLANTA	.304	97	303	54	92	6	14	8	28	18	52	26
1993	ATLANTA	.276	95	272	42	75	18	6	6	28	16	42	19
1994	ATLANTA	.288	46	191	32	55	10	0	4	21	16	28	19
	CINCINNATI	.277	46	184	26	51	7	4	0	7	16	35	19
1995	CINCINNATI	.240	33	129	19	31	2	3	1	10	9	18	16
	SAN FRANCISCO	.285	52	214	29	61	9	5	5	18	18	42	8
Minor League Totals		.282	182	708	122	200	34	15	13	70	64	126	68
Major League Totals		.264	494	1,583	249	418	57	36	33	141	121	275	127

POSTSEASON BASEBALL STATS

National League Championship Series

Year	Opponent	Games	At-Bats	Runs	Hits	Avg.	Home Runs	RBI	Stolen Bases
1992	Pirates	4	5	0	0	0	0	0	0

World Series

Year	Opponent	Games	At-Bats	Runs	Hits	Avg.	Home Runs	RBI	Stolen Bases
1992	Blue Jays	4	15	4	8	.533	0	1	5

REGULAR SEASON NFL STATS

	TACKLES	DEFENSE PASSES DEF.	INT.	YDS.	TD	PUNT RETURNS NO.	AVG.	TD	KICKOFF RETURNS NO.	AVG.	TD	RECEIVING NO.	AVG.	TD.
1989 (Atl.)	39	8	5	52	0	28	11.0	1	35	20.7	0	1	-8.0	0
1990	50	18	3	153	2	29	8.6	1	39	21.8	0	-	-	-
1991	49	14	6	119	1	21	8.1	0	26	22.2	1	1	17.0	0
1992	66	4	3	105	0	13	3.2	0	40	26.7	2	3	15.0	1
1993	34	8	7	91	0	2	10.5	0	7	24.1	0	6	17.7	1
1994 (S.F.)	37	15	6	303	3	-	-	-	-	-	-	-	-	-
1995 (Dallas)	28	10	2	34	1	1	54.0	0	1	15.0	0	2	12.5	0
Totals	303	77	32	857	7	94	9.0	2	148	23.0	3	13	14.2	2

POSTSEASON NFL STATS

	TACKLES	DEFENSE PASSES DEF.	INT.	YDS.	TD	PUNT RETURNS NO.	AVG.	TD	KICKOFF RETURNS NO.	AVG.	TD	RECEIVING NO.	AVG.	TD.
1991 (Alt.)	10	2	1	31	0	3	11.0	0	6	20.7	0	-	-	-
1994 (S.F.)	6	7	2	15	0	-	-	-	1	25.0	0	-	-	-
1995 (Dal.)	7	3	1	12	0	4	9.5	0	-	-	-	3	31.7	0
Totals	23	12	4	58	0	7	10.1	0	7	21.3	0	3	31.7	0

93

BRETT FAVRE

COLLEGE STATS

	PASSING							RUSHING			
	ATT.	COMP.	YDS.	PCT.	TD	INT.	LONG	ATT.	YDS.	TD	LONG
1987	194	79	1264	40.7	15	13	63	57	169	1	35
1988	345	193	2428	55.9	17	5	48	58	-7	0	32
1989	381	206	2588	54.0	14	10	80	43	-25	0	32
1990	314	178	1913	56.7	9	7	62	47	-233	0	6
Totals	1234	656	8193	53.1	55	35	80	205	-96	1	35

REGULAR SEASON STATS

	PASSING							RUSHING			
	ATT.	COMP.	YDS.	PCT.	TD	INT.	RATING	ATT.	YDS.	AVG.	TD
1991(Atl)	5	0	0	0.0	0	2	0.0	0	0	0	0
1992(GB)	471	302	3227	64.1	18	13	85.3	47	198	4.2	1
1993	522	318	3303	60.9	19	24	72.2	58	216	3.7	1
1994	582	363	3882	62.4	33	14	90.7	42	202	4.8	2
1995	570	359	4413	63.0	38	13	99.5	39	181	4.6	3
Totals	2150	1342	14,825	62.4	108	66	86.8	186	797	4.3	7

POSTSEASON STATS

	PASSING							RUSHING			
	ATT.	COMP.	YDS.	PCT.	TD	INT.	RATING	ATT.	YDS.	AVG.	TD
1993	71	43	535	60.5	5	2	89.8	4	18	4.5	0
1994	73	41	473	56.1	0	1	70.2	4	7	1.8	0
1995	102	66	805	64.7	8	2	106.9	7	7	1.0	0
Totals	246	167	1813	61.0	13	5	91.1	15	32	2.1	0

If you enjoyed this book, you might want to order some of our other exciting titles:

BASKETBALL SUPERSTARS ALBUM 1996, Richard J. Brenner. Includes 16 full-color pages, and mini-bios of the game's top superstars, plus career and all-time stats. 48 pages.

MICHAEL JORDAN * MAGIC JOHNSON, by Richard J. Brenner. A dual biography of two of the greatest superstars of all time. 128 pages, 15 dynamite photos.

ANFERNEE HARDAWAY * GRANT HILL, by Brian Cazeneuve. A dual biography of two of the brightest young stars in basketball. 96 pages, 10 pages of photos.

SHAQUILLE O'NEAL * LARRY JOHNSON, by Richard J. Brenner. A dual biography of two of the brightest young stars in basketball. 96 pages, 10 pages of photos.

PRO FOOTBALL'S ALL-TIME ALL-STAR TEAM, by Richard J. Brenner. The top 24 football players of all time are profiled in this photo-filled book. 128 pages.

STEVE YOUNG * JERRY RICE, by Richard J. Brenner. A dual biography of the two superstars who led the 49ers to the Super Bowl. 96 pages, 10 pages of photos.

TROY AIKMAN * STEVE YOUNG, by Richard J. Brenner. A dual biography of the top two quarterbacks in the NFL. 96 pages, 10 pages of photos.

GREG MADDUX * CAL RIPKEN, JR., by Richard J. Brenner. A dual biography of two future Hall of Famers. 96 pages, 10 pages of photos.

KEN GRIFFEY JR. * FRANK THOMAS, by Brian Cazeneuve. A dual biography of two of baseball's brightest young superstars. 96 pages, 10 pages of photos.

MARIO LEMIEUX, by Richard J. Brenner. An exciting biography of one of hockey's all-time greats. 96 pages, 10 pages of photos.

THE WORLD SERIES, THE GREAT CONTESTS, by Richard J. Brenner. The special excitement of the Fall Classic is brought to life through seven of the most thrilling Series ever played, including 1993. 176 pages, including 16 action-packed photos.

MICHAEL JORDAN, by Richard J. Brenner. An easy-to-read, photo-filled biography especially for younger readers. 32 pages.

GRANT HILL, by Richard J. Brenner. An easy-to-read, photo-filled biography especially for younger readers. 32 pages.

SHAQUILLE O'NEAL, by Richard J. Brenner. An easy-to-read, photo-filled biography especially for younger readers. 32 pages.

WAYNE GRETZKY, by Richard J. Brenner. An easy-to-read, photo-filled biography especially for younger readers. 32 pages.

TOUCHDOWN! THE FOOTBALL FUN BOOK, by Richard J. Brenner. Trivia, puzzles, mazes and much more! 64 pages.

PLEASE SEE NEXT PAGE FOR ORDER FORM

ORDER FORM

Payment must accompany all orders and must be in U.S. dollars.

Postage and handling is $1.35 per book up to a maximum of $6.75 ($1.75 to a maximum of $8.75 in Canada).

Mr. Brenner will personally autograph his books for an additional cost of $1.00 per book.

Please send me the following books:

No. of copies	Title	Price
_____	BASKETBALL SUPERSTARS ALBUM 1996	$4.50/$6.25 Can.
_____	MICHAEL JORDAN * MAGIC JOHNSON	$3.50/$4.25 Can.
_____	ANFERNEE HARDAWAY * GRANT HILL	$3.99/$5.50 Can.
_____	SHAQUILLE O'NEAL * LARRY JOHNSON	$3.50/$4.50 Can.
_____	PRO FOOTBALL'S ALL-TIME ALL-STAR TEAM	$4.50/$5.50 Can.
_____	DEION SANDERS*BRETT FAVRE	$3.99/$5.50 Can.
_____	STEVE YOUNG * JERRY RICE	$3.99/$5.50 Can.
_____	TROY AIKMAN * STEVE YOUNG	$3.50/$4.50 Can.
_____	GREG MADDUX * CAL RIPKEN, JR.	$3.99/$5.50 Can.
_____	KEN GRIFFEY JR. * FRANK THOMAS	$3.50/$4.50 Can.
_____	MARIO LEMIEUX	$3.50/$4.50 Can.
_____	THE WORLD SERIES, THE GREAT CONTESTS	$4.50/$5.50 Can.
_____	MICHAEL JORDAN	$4.00/$5.50 Can.
_____	GRANT HILL	$3.50/$4.50 Can.
_____	SHAQUILLE O'NEAL	$3.25/$4.50 Can.
_____	WAYNE GRETZKY	$3.25/$4.50 Can.
_____	TOUCHDOWN! THE FOOTBALL FUN BOOK	$3.50/$5.00 Can.

TOTAL NUMBER OF BOOKS ORDERED _____

TOTAL PRICE OF BOOKS $_____

POSTAGE AND HANDLING $_____

AUTOGRAPHING COST $_____

TOTAL PAYMENT ENCLOSED $_____

NAME _____

ADDRESS _____ ST. JOSEPH CATHOLIC SCHOOL _____
188 Lucinda Lane
CITY _____ Watervliet, MI 49098 STATE _____ ZIP _____ COUNTRY _____

Send to: East End Publishing, 54 Alexander Drive, Syosset NY 11791 USA. Dept. TD. Allow three weeks for delivery. Discounts are available on orders of 25 or more copies. For details call (516) 364-6383.